W9-CTI-410

KATHLEEN'S VINEYARD

The Fetzer Family Matriarch
Shares Her Story

KATHLEEN FETZER
with SARAH SUGGS

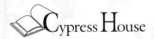

Cypress House

Illustration by Daniel Fetzer

Kathleen's Vineyard: The Fetzer Family Matriarch Shares Her Story
Copyright © 2005 by Kathleen Fetzer
www.fetzerfoundation.org

Cypress House
155 Cypress Street
Fort Bragg, CA 95437
(800) 773-7782
www.cypresshouse.com

Cover and book design: Michael Brechner / Cypress House

Robert Benson interview reprinted from *Great Winemakers of California: Conversations with Robert Benson* (Capra Press, 1977) with the kind permission of Robert Benson.

Library of Congress Cataloging-in-Publication Data

Fetzer, Kathleen, 1921-
Kathleen's vineyard : the Fetzer family matriarch shares her story / Kathleen Fetzer with Sarah Suggs. -- 1st ed.
p. cm.
Includes bibliographical references and index.
ISBN 1-879384-58-2 (casebound : alk. paper)
1. Fetzer, Kathleen, 1921- 2. Vintners--California--Biography.
3. Fetzer family. 4. Wine and wine making--California--History.
I. Suggs, Sarah. II. Title.
TP547.F48A3 2005
641.2'2'0922794--dc22   2004015262

Printed in Canada

2 4 6 8 9 7 5 3 1

DEDICATION

This book is dedicated to my late husband and father of our eleven children, Bernard "Barney" Fetzer, who was an inspriation to me and to those he loved.

ACKNOWLEDGMENTS

I want to express my appreciation to those who contributed to my book. The week after September 11, 2001, Sarah Suggs, whom I've known for many years, visited me. As many people know, that period of time gave pause to our nation and helped us to realize what is truly important in life, our loved ones. During that week, we began reviewing and sorting my favorite recipes with the goal of creating a cookbook. As the work continued and we discussed how these recipes were used for many years in raising my children, we began work on my biography as well. Sarah and I worked together for over three years, and it was a labor of love.

I also want to thank my daughter Kathleen Mary Fetzer, who oversees the Fetzer Family Foundation, which will benefit from the proceeds of this book and support many charitable causes.

Katrina Fetzer, my granddaughter, helped us archive our family photos. Dorothy McKay, who facilitated my oral history in 1991, which proved to be enormously helpful. Nicholas Ores my attorney, and his wife Fran, who helped me establish my foundation.

And of course, each of my eleven children, John, Kathy, Joey, Jim, Patti, Mary, Diana, Bobby, Richie, Teresa and Danny, who provided encouragement and support throughout this project.

CONTENTS

KATHLEEN'S VINEYARD

MINNESOTA UPBRINGING

Old Schoolhouse. Kathleen is in the front row, second from the left.

I was born in Luverne, Minnesota on November 2, 1921, and attended a one-room schoolhouse known as The Little White Schoolhouse in the Country.

One of my earliest childhood recollections is the birth of my little brother John. I was about six years old, and my older sister, Monica, took care of my siblings and me. All of us had been born at home, and John was the first to be born in a hospital. Monica watched over my sisters, Betty and Jean, and my brother, Homer, and me. Eventually, there were ten of us. With five brothers and four sisters, I was right in the middle.

Growing up in Minnesota meant being raised around many lakes — "the land of 10,000 lakes," to be exact. We lived near Lake Benton, and a river ran through our property. We swam in the swimming hole in the summer, and skated on the frozen river during winter. We skied at home, holding tightly to the reins of our horses, which would pull us along behind. It was a unique way to ski, and a unique way to have lots of fun.

In later years, we moved to Pipestone, about thirty-five miles from Luverne. My father had a cattle ranch that sat on a section of land that was about one square mile. A road divided our property, the barns on one side of it, and our house on the other. We had several barn buildings: a cob-house, a seed-corn house, and an icehouse. In the winter we would cut ice and place it in the icehouse, then cover it with sawdust piled high. The ice would last us all the way through summer!

We used to play hide-and-go-seek in the corn house, where my dad would wrap seed corn in cloth to see if it was going to sprout, and then plant it if it did. Eventually, there would be long cornrows, which made a perfect place to play our favorite childhood games. We played cards a lot: rummy, pinochle, and five hundred; to this day, I still love to play cards.

Thanksgiving and Christmas brought special memories. We had a turkey at Thanksgiving, and my mother fixed a goose, too. We would

… in those years, we didn't have enough money to go to town and buy ornaments.

Kathleen's Parents, Philetta and John

bake pumpkin pies and prepare cranberries, not unlike today. I started cooking early with my mother. She taught me how to use spices, but not so much as to take away from the natural taste of what was being prepared. For roasting, she would rub a clove of garlic around the inside of a cast-iron Dutch oven. I still don't like using a lot of garlic, but prefer a hint of it, as my mother taught me. I started baking when I was eight, making yeast breads, using a great big dishpan to make them.

We didn't have a lot of fir trees where we lived, which was in the southwest corner of Minnesota, near Sioux Falls and South Dakota. One day, we went out to cut a branch off of a tree. We stood it upright, just like a Christmas tree, and decorated it with popcorn, loop rings, and other homemade decorations—in those years, we didn't have enough money to go to town and buy ornaments.

On the Fourth of July, my father would go buy soda pop and five gallons of ice cream, which was how we celebrated the Fourth of July. We never had soda pop except for that day!

Growing up, I always dreamed of marrying a singing cowboy. In those years, we didn't have much, especially living on a farm in a small town.

My Aunt Cora and Uncle Oscar would come to visit, and Aunt Cora would take me home with her afterward. I guess she thought taking one child off of my mother's hands would be helpful, so she chose me. Maybe she thought I took after her, because she was a seamstress, something we had in common.

My mother, Philetta Canfield, was wonderful. I always felt I could go and talk to her. She sewed, did all the cooking and canning, took care of the house, and cared for us children. My father, John Frank Kohn, was in the service during World War I. In his youth, he played baseball for a team in Iowa. Later, he worked in a bank, and then became a farmer. He was a hardworking man and provided well for his family, though I can remember some hard times, especially during the Depression, when he lost the family farm. My grandfather had given each of his sons a farm as a wedding gift, and both farms were lost during those difficult years. As a result, we moved to Pipestone, Minnesota, where we rented a farm. We always had food to eat and a place to live.

Mother would ride to town in a buggy to buy staples like flour, sugar, and coffee. Others could buy butter and grapefruit, but for the most part, we lived off of our land. We would butcher a pig, we had beef regularly, and our chickens laid eggs—in all, we were lucky.

My paternal grandfather, Frank Kohn, lived in Lucerne where I was born. He was German. He had a big, white house with a porch that went all around the sides. Grandfather liked wine, especially port.

I attended Pipestone High School, which was a nice, average-size school. We lived miles out of town, so I rode the bus. The ride was so far that I decided to stay closer to school, work to earn my room and board, and go home on weekends to visit my family. I worked for a relative who had a beauty shop, then worked for Don and Joy Hart, who owned a grocery store and then owned the town newspaper, the *Pipestone Star.* I cleaned house for the Harts and took care of their little boy Dale. Years later, after I'd moved, Joy had a second child, and named her Kathleen.

I liked high school. I loved geography and enjoyed penmanship, which was well taught in those days. I studied home economics and sewing, too, using the skills I had learned at home. I began sewing when I was very young, and enjoyed sewing dresses for my little sisters.

Kathleen with Uncle Oscar Upsetta

3

I knew so much about the subject that the teacher would ask me to help other sewing students. On special occasions, we were allowed to dance in the gymnasium at noon. I wore a pretty yellow dress to my prom—one of the few dresses I didn't make myself.

World War II was starting, so many men were joining the service. Everyone was leaving, and my older sister, Lois, suggested that my girlfriend and I move to California to join her.

My life would never be the same.

The Girls

Back row: *Mother, Monica, and Lois.* Front row: *Betty, Jean, and Kathleen*

SINGLE DAYS IN SAN FRANCISCO BAY

Leaving Minnesota, my mother and father gave me some advice: "We have taught you all the morals and the things in life that should be valuable to you. Just remember to avoid letting people talk you into things. Use your own judgment." I followed that advice for the rest of my life. Dad bought a thousand-dollar life insurance policy as my high school graduation gift. I was ready for my move to California.

Lois and her husband, Lee, lived in Oakland, California during World War II. Lee served in the navy there. I was excited to arrive from Minnesota with my girlfriend Billie Riche. At the Oakland station, Lee picked us up in a little car he owned. Oakland was a beautiful city, full of sun. I lived with Billie at

Oakland apartment building and sign for Bellini's Restaurant

the corner of 41st Street and Telegraph, near Bellini's restaurant. The manager of the nearby Fox Theater lived in our building, and we rented our apartment from him. Each day, I took the trolley to go to work for Miller Meat Packing Company in Oakland. The army took over operations while I was there, and all of the meat went to feed the troops. My boss was a nice lady named Flo, and she and I had a good relationship. Flo would often ask my opinion when she was considering hiring a new girl. She felt I was down to earth and had good intuition. Flo lived near Lake Merritt in Oakland. She was single for many years, before she married and moved to Redding.

My girlfriends and I would shop at Capwell's, Liberty House, and other stores in San Francisco. We used the Key System, a transportation system that coordinated tram, electric train, and ferry schedules in the Bay Area. Every weekend, we would to go San Francisco to shop, and then, in the evening, go to a dance at El Patio, at the end of Market Street. The gentlemen would come and invite us to dance right away. Men would come up and ask if they could have the first dance, and I usually answered, "You may have the second."

We joined the USO and the YWCA, went to dances, and served lemonade and cookies. The other girls and I would try teaching the servicemen to dance, which was great fun. I especially enjoyed the jitterbug, and also loved to waltz. When servicemen from back home in Minnesota were coming to town, we would hear from their folks, and invite them to the dances.

Later, two other girlfriends from Pipestone, Lorna and Ruth Halling, joined us. When the manager of the Fox Theater retired, he arranged it so that we could rent his apartment, which gave us two extra bedrooms. We bought all of our furniture for 200 dollars. We had a dining room table, a front room, and a sun porch. We fixed the porch into a

bedroom, and when Billie's brother married, we rented the extra room to his wife and him while he was in the service there.

Everyone was together in a family-like setting. My sister, Betty, stayed with Lois and Lee. Beth, Lee's sister, stayed with her sister, Fern, and we all lived close by one another. We were having fun, even though there was a war going on.

We loved going to dances, and it was at a popular dance hall, Sweets, that I met a serviceman who made a big impression on me—Bernard Alexander "Barney" Fetzer.

Kathleen — The Oakland years

My Courtship with Barney

I n November, Lois and Lee informed us that they would be hosting Thanksgiving at their home. It was a little place, but they wanted each of us girls, Betty, Billie, Beth, and me, to invite a serviceman to Thanksgiving dinner. Each of us was given a dinner assignment—I baked the pies. I had just met Barney, and I decided to invite him. He didn't really want to come, because he thought it would be a family affair and that there might be too many people. He finally decided to join us, but I found out later that he nearly didn't. He used the Key System to get to the dinner, and Lee, a teaser, joked with Barney that he was late and almost didn't make it.

Shortly after Thanksgiving, Barney shipped out on a merchant ship. I didn't see him again until Christmastime. He called and told me he'd bought me something for Christmas. It was a rosary, which I have to this day. Along with the rosary, he also gave me a little blue fob, a bow with a small round locket that had a rose in the center of a blue background. Barney put his picture in the locket.

On our first date, Barney took me to dance at the Claremont Hotel in Berkeley. The doors to the verandah were opened and we danced outside to the music of the big band. Barney didn't like to dance as much as I, but dance we did. Barney shipped out again shortly afterward. His brother, Jerry, was onshore in the Coast Guard, and Barney asked him come by to tell me that he had shipped

Barney Fetzer

out and couldn't call me. That's the way it was during those years.

I didn't have other boyfriends at that time, but went to dances with my girlfriends. I really liked Barney a lot, but I didn't get to see him much. When his ship would come in, I would receive lots of letters and he would get mine. One night, Jerry took me to Bertoli's before he had to return to the East Coast. All three Fetzer boys were in the service, both Barney and Bob in the Merchant Marine. Barney loved to read, and took all his books out to sea. He went around the world a couple of times during the war, and I worried about him.

In 1945, when the war ended, Barney went home to Los Angeles to see his mother. He called from there to let me know he was coming north. He told me he had passed through Oregon during his time in the service, and wanted to go to Klamath Falls.

When he arrived in Oakland and came to see me, he asked me to marry him and come to Oregon. At the time, I said, "You'd better ask my dad." He spoke with my father, who told him yes, "On one condition: that you'll always take care of her."

"Yes, I will," Barney replied. It was a promise he would keep.

MARRIED IN OREGON

I boarded the train alone in Oakland, bound for Klamath Falls. I was excited, and really nervous, because I had never traveled alone and didn't know a soul in Oregon other than Barney. I took comfort in knowing that he was very polite and gentle, and it made me more comfortable to know that he was a man of faith—his first gift to me had been a rosary. Anxious to see my future husband, I wondered if I would get there on time. Barney picked me up at the train station, and that evening he presented me an engagement ring. He took me to his little apartment, which was to be my temporary home, while he rented a separate room to live in before we got married. That's how strict we were in those days—no living together before marriage.

In those early days, Barney worked for an insurance agency owned by the Roycroft family. On the snowy morning of December 5, 1945, at an eight o'clock mass attended by the faithful, we were married at Sacred Heart Roman Catholic Church, the Roycrofts serving as our best man and matron of honor. I wore a pale yellow suit, a matching feathered hat, and a corsage. Afterward, we celebrated with the Roycrofts at breakfast in the big hotel in Klamath Falls.

For our honeymoon, we motored to Ashland, driving on the treacherous Green Springs Road. It was quite an adventure, as it was snowing at the time, which made the roads dangerous. We stayed at a small, romantic inn that boasted a water fountain with mineral water. Unfortunately, even though it was said to be good for your health, it tasted terrible!

One night, Barney and I woke up to shouts of "Fire!" in the hotel. We were told to exit down the stairs and out into the snow, which we did. Eventually, the fire was extinguished and we were allowed to return—it was a very scary chapter of our honeymoon!

Mr. and Mrs. Kohn

Barney and I hadn't had much time to spend together during our courtship, so our honeymoon was a time for us to discover a lot of things about each other. Barney was a quiet man. He did not have the "gift of gab" like some men, but I preferred his conservative style. He was thoughtful and enjoyed classical music and painting, though he found precious little time to paint, especially when we started our family. He was genuine and caring, which became even more evident as the years went on.

RAISED WITH RELIGION

My father was a Roman Catholic, and my mother converted to that religion. She was a very good Catholic, and made certain that we were brought up accordingly. There was no Catholic school in Pipestone, so I attended catechism, and had my first Holy Communion and Confirmation.

In our family, we all went to church. Dad would go out to the car and honk the horn and everybody had better come a-running! Boy, we were expected to be ready when we heard that horn toot. We all piled in the Studebaker and off we went.

Growing up, Barney always went to church with his family. We passed our faith on to our children, too. Each of them was baptized and raised Catholic. In later years, I learned how much my religion meant to me; I don't know how I could have coped with many things that occurred. When things get tough, I say my Rosary. If I wake up in the middle of the night and can't find it, I just count on my fingers. The Blessed Virgin Mary means a lot to me. I wonder if people underestimate religion today. If you have no faith, what is there to guide you, especially during challenging times?

Our First Home

While Barney was anticipating my arrival in Oregon, he bought a surprise wedding gift—a little one-bedroom house. He paid $2,000 for it, and it even had furniture! I'd sold all of my furniture in Oakland for about $100. In all, I went to Oregon with $200 in my pocket, which we used to buy our first refrigerator.

Before leaving Oakland, my girlfriends gave me a bridal shower that included a set of wineglasses. Of all their gifts, I remember that set of glassware the most.

It was exciting to be in our first house, and decorate it as I wanted. It was a cute little house. The bathroom had a bathtub, toilet, and sink, but the sink wasn't connected, so we used a basin underneath! We never did get the sink connected during the time we lived there.

There was a long front room, which was living and dining room combined, and one bedroom. Those were fun times. One day, our kitchen pipes froze and broke. Cold water was flowing all over and out of the house. I'll never forget it! That was when we decided to move to a warmer town in Oregon—Medford.

Barney and Kathleen at their first home

Becoming A Mother

It wasn't long before I was expecting our first baby. Soon I was knitting and crocheting and preparing for the arrival. In December, my eighth month, Barney and I walked to church one day. It was an icy morning, and even though Barney was holding my arm, I slipped and, though I didn't fall to the ground, my body felt a sudden jerk. I began feeling labor pains, so Barney rushed me to the hospital, where I had our son John. When they gave him to me, they had not removed all of his mucus, and he was choking. Scared, I rang for the nurse, insisting that they come and take him to clear his passages.

In those days, women stayed in the hospital about a week. I was hardly allowed to get out of bed! When I finally went home with the baby, I was afraid he wouldn't breathe at night, so I placed his bassinet right next to our bed.

Barney was so excited to be a father, and it was such a miracle to have a baby. At night when I would go to bed, I would say to myself, "God takes care of them at night. He is going to breathe. That's the way it's going to be."

When I became pregnant with our second child, Kathleen, I had a sudden attack of appendicitis in my seventh month. Barney rushed me to the emergency room. As we arrived, a robbery was taking place at the hospital! As I was prepared for the operation, I was told they could save the baby or me, and that they would try to save me. It was against my wishes—I wanted them to save the baby. During the surgery, I was given injections to keep me from going into labor. Somehow, they were able to remove my appendix and prevent an early delivery. No sooner was I recovering from surgery, than I developed pneumonia and became deathly ill. It was so serious that my parents were summoned from Minnesota. Friends and relatives from San Francisco came to see me—perhaps for the last time.

John and Kathy

I had a private nurse night and day, a wonderful lady who happened to be Roman Catholic. One day, she entered my room with a bundle that the hospital was going to throw away. It was a baby that had died, and she had swaddled it in blankets. She asked me if she could leave the infant in my room while she called a priest to find out what to do. It was a strange and difficult thing to deal with at that point. The nurse simply didn't want to throw the baby away. Soon after that, I experienced the most critical night of my life.

❧

A Miraculous Night

I felt like I was slipping away and was going to die. I found myself climbing steps—cathedral steps. As I crawled up and up toward the top, I saw lights; everything seemed brilliantly lit. At the very top was a little boy. It was my friend Rita's son, Jimmy, who had drowned earlier during my pregnancy. He was about two years old, and fell into an irrigation ditch near his home. It was terribly hard on Rita, but despite her state of mourning,

She asked me if she could leave the infant in my room while she called a priest to find out what to do.

she took care of baby John while I was hospitalized.

When I finally reached the top of the cathedral steps, there was Jimmy, saying, "Go back! Go back!" All of a sudden, I was awake in my hospital bed, choking on the mucus that had filled my lungs. My nurse was with me and she helped me, literally pulling the mucus out of my throat. After that, I began to feel better and my condition improved.

After a few days, I went into labor. I had been given ether for my earlier surgery, and they didn't want to give me any other drugs, so I had the baby naturally. Though not a Catholic, my physician, Dr. Massey, told me that it was a pure miracle—he hadn't expected me to live.

Barney called my parents in Minnesota and told them I was doing fine and that there was no need for them to come. They cashed in their train tickets and sent us the money to help pay the hospital bills. While I was in the hospital, John had his first birthday. Rita took a picture of him in his high chair next to her little girl Susan. Rita baked a birthday cake for him and visited me in the hospital, bringing the picture of John. He was my firstborn, so it was pretty hard for me not to be there to celebrate. I begged the doctor to let me go home. He said, "You can go home if you have help." We didn't have money, though, to pay someone. Barney was selling insurance at that time, and was able to pay the doctor's bill. The hospital bill was nearly a thousand dollars, which was a lot of money then.

Kathleen, our new baby, remained in the hospital for about a month, and that gave me a chance to rest a little at home. Recovering from pneumonia took a long time, not to mention recuperating from appendicitis and surgery. Soon after, I became pregnant with our third child, but lost the baby early in the pregnancy—I hadn't fully regained my health and didn't have much strength.

Kathy and John were like twins; they even looked alike. Our friends, the Jollys, had twin girls, and when we went out together with our children, Kathy and John resembled twins more that their two daughters did! Today, as the eldest children, Kathy and John remain very close.

As a child, John went through a period where he would color everything in dark colors, which worried me. I asked the doctor if it was anything to be concerned about, and he said, "All you have to do is hand him a bright crayon." Soon, John was coloring rainbows!

Barney, My Helpmate

Barney was a great help to me, but would you believe that children made him nervous? It was partly my fault, because I didn't give him more to do with the kids. I felt I wanted to take care of the children.

Barney helped with the cooking and the washing. We had a washing machine, but no dryer. One day, I hung diapers outside so the sun could bleach them white. Instead, they froze in the cold weather!

Barney decided to build a new house in Medford, and I was to have a washer and dryer. It was a flat-top house, popular at the time, with two bedrooms, a kitchen, and a combination living/dining room. Later, we enclosed the carport and made a rumpus room, and added a third bedroom lined in cedar. I became pregnant with Joey, and we

had four of our children in Medford—Joey, Jimmy, Patti and Mary—all born at Sacred Heart Hospital.

Barney decided to change careers. After selling insurance, he became an accountant, working for Stagecoach Orchards. Barney had done well selling insurance, even winning a trip to Victoria, British Columbia. Still, it was after the war, and not too many people were buying insurance. After a time, he rose to become a controller at Medford Door, a door-manufacturing plant.

Motherhood in Full Bloom

I enjoyed being a mother, and enjoy it to this day. That was my life: I liked to cook, sew, decorate… the job was never done.

All of our children were very lucky because they were healthy. I suppose they have strong genes. Jimmy was more of a blond, like my father, and had blue eyes. His hair got darker in later years; and all of my other children had dark eyes.

When I had so many boys, the doctor would ask how they were getting along. I told him, "I'm worried because they fight." He replied, "If they didn't fight, you'd worry more!" He made me laugh. Still, I worried about their squabbling and always tried to teach them not to bicker.

The girls were a great help. Kathleen was the little mother, the girls would often take over with John. That's one of the blessings of a large family—you always have help. They would hang clothes, or do whatever chores needed doing. If I needed to do something, I could ask one to watch the others.

John started school in Medford. I had taught him not to fight, but some boys from school would knock his lunch pail out of his hand when he was walking home from school, and twice they broke his thermos.

"You have to stop this," Barney said. Just give it to them if they try to knock your lunch pail down." Evidently, John did, because we never had any more trouble! We taught our children to hold their own. I didn't have any problems with the younger children, because they could call on their brothers to help. The older children always protected the little ones in school.

My kids thought I had eyes in the back of my head. I bought books with stories about stealing, lying, and other subjects. There might be a story about telling the truth, and sure enough, they would finally confess to any wrongdoing. I would read these stories to the little ones at night, after bath time, while the older kids did the dishes.

If I ever heard a sassy mouth, I would take my Ivory soap and threaten to wash out their mouths! They didn't like that very much, but it made them straighten up and behave. I wanted my children to know that I was the boss. Today, they are all healthy and happy—all eleven of them.

California Bound

After several years in Medford, Barney received two offers of accounting work in California: one in Cloverdale and one in Ukiah. As it happened, he preferred Ukiah, because it had a Catholic school, so Barney chose Hollow Tree Lumber, owned by Bill Smith and Bill Morris.

I was pregnant with our seventh child, Robert, when we made the move from Redding. Due to my pregnancy, it was a hard move, but Hollow Tree Lumber hired movers to pack our household, which really helped. They packed and unpacked everything, and even put away everything in the cupboards!

Taking a road trip to with six kids was quite an adventure. On the way to our new home in California, Barney got the idea to stop and take a break with the kids. He made a slingshot for the boys, and they had fun trying their new toy. Then, we all got into the station wagon and continued our journey.

In Ukiah, we rented a large house owned by the Sandlins—who were the proprietors of the Palace Hotel in town—for six months, while our home was being built in a subdivision called Regina Heights in the hills of Ukiah. The Sandlins were so kind that they even allowed me to use a beautiful bassinet when I gave birth to Bobby shortly after our move. When we moved into our own home, I left the bassinet there as the Sandlins instructed, and was saddened to learn that someone broke into the empty house and stole the bassinet.

Our house in Regina Heights was such a pretty place, especially because it had so many trees, and Barney planted the backyard with begonias and other beautiful flowers. The children were becoming accustomed to the climate, and Mary's asthma was cured, though Kathy and Jimmy still had occasional bouts. The children were enrolled at St. Mary's, and rode their bikes to school. While we lived in Regina Heights, another daughter, Diana, was born.

We made many friends in our home. A next-door neighbor befriended Barney and they began to play chess. It turns out the neighbor was in the real estate business, and one day he told Barney about a property in Redwood Valley. It was to become the home ranch of a business Barney would someday begin—Fetzer Vineyards.

The Home Ranch

Shortly after Diana was born, Barney wanted a larger place, maybe a ranch, for the family. He was always on the lookout for places that would suit us. On one occasion, his chess partner told Barney about an 800-acre ranch that had come on the market. It was the Jay Lee Smith Ranch he wanted Barney to go and see, which Barney did.

Barney was really taken with the property and wanted

to buy it. Someone had already put money down, so he thought he had no chance of owning the ranch. As fate would have it, the loan didn't go through and it became available again. Barney talked to me about it, and we decided we would buy it.

Barney helped me into the car and off we went to see the ranch. We drove into the driveway and what do you think I first laid eyes on? Weeds, weeds, and more weeds! Goodness, everything was run down, including the house. The owners of Hollow Tree Lumber came out to look at the ranch and told Barney, "We're sure you'll tear this house down." Compared to our neat and tidy home in Regina Heights, I thought, Oh, my gosh—we've surely got our work cut out for us. I was not about to move into that house in its present condition, so Barney and our eldest son, John, started working to improve it and make it ready for the family.

Barney would work all day at the lumber company, and after the day's end, he, John, and sometimes Joey would work much of the night, and even sleep over there. They started to fix the kitchen first. Barney built all the cupboards. There was funny-looking wallpaper,

On one occasion, his chess partner told Barney about an 800-acre ranch that had come on the market.

and the windows had red-white-and-blue-striped drapes. Barney had a little camp stove and would cook hominy for the boys. At night they could hear the field mice running around, so they had company.

Barney could envision the future more than I could, and it motivated him. Some days I would see progress and say, "I'll bring some of my lawn furniture out." Then I'd become discouraged and take it all back. Eventually, on the Fourth of July, the house was ready for move-in. On that move, I was eight months pregnant with Richard, our eighth child. My two brothers came to help Barney move. My

brother, John, was working for Sears and had a trolley, which came in handy. They would deliver a truckload of bedroom furniture, and by the time they came back with the next load, I had the bedroom all ready, in time for the kids to go to sleep that night. So, we moved from a brand-new home in Regina Heights to a run-down ranch in Redwood Valley. Barney was so unsure whether I was going to be happy, that he rented the house in Regina Heights in case we had to move back. That move was the hardest ever, but we made it.

THE START

I wanted to support Barney in his goals for make a living. He worried, but he never burdened me with it. I was the type of person who saved and saved as much as I could. I did all the baking and cooking and sewed for the kids. Barney continued working for the lumber company, and was fortunate to buy lumber very cheaply for building.

Barney was very optimistic. When we started and moved to the ranch, we had grapevines, old tractors, and equipment. We also had Fritz Fernbach, who sort of came with the ranch. For-

We drove into the driveway and what do you think I first laid eyes on? Weeds, weeds, and more weeds!

merly a mechanic for Buick, he fixed the tractors and all the equipment for us. He was always at the ranch working on the weekends.

To keep the grapes, I would go out and prune with the boys while Kathy would watch the kids in the house. It was so nice to be in the beautiful vineyards, especially in the spring. John would drive the tractor, and Barney would work, too. Everybody helped: if it hadn't been for the children, we could never have done it. They learned a view of life from their dad: "If you work hard, you can make it."

When we were getting started, even the bankers would say, "Oh, golly, you're making a big jump, going into the wine business!" Barney had done his homework, however, and calculated that he could make more money selling wine by the bottle than he could by selling grapes. Barney always had everything planned; he had ledgers that show how far ahead he would plan things. Now, John does that, too. You know there will be changes, but the planning helps you be prepared.

We kept improving the house, and things came together little by little. All of the kids had to work. I would go out to the fields to help with the pruning and to keep the boys

THE WINERY

in the field—because Joe and Jimmy would go off to the creek to play!

Barney still worked at the lumber company, and on weekends rode the tractor. When John became sixteen, he got a driver's license, and Barney bought him a car so he could drive the kids back and forth to school at St. Mary's. It was a great help.

When we first moved to Redwood Valley, we worked to pick the grapes from our old vineyards, then deliver them to Allied Grape Growers, in Ukiah. They were a part of an old winery in Cloverdale—a former mission. All the grapes they bought were dumped together and mixed. That started Barney

The new improved Home Ranch

thinking, Gee! Why not keep them separate and produce varietal wines? After a couple of years, we started to sell the grapes to wine hobbyists, selling to Washington, New York, and Los Angeles, and shipping in airtight, lined freight boxes. Eventually, the hobbyists started bringing their wine back to us to taste. Barney said, "Well, gee, if they can make wine, we can make wine, too."

Barney went to the university at Berkeley, and studied with them as to what to grow. They decided that cabernet grapes would grow well up here, so we began planting a lot of cabernet. It was a slow process. We had one little building. We started with five stainless steel tanks—and we thought we had a lot. We started our little winery with a few barrels from France.

Barney's accounting background helped a great deal. He loved to read, and he was such a studious person, always with a book in his hands, that it seemed he was studying constantly. He would sometimes bring a book to the breakfast table, and I would say, "You shouldn't read at the table."

Each year, we would take out one of the old vineyards and plant a new one. That's how we started, adding another part of the winery year by year.

Original Fetzer label

Expanding Fetzer Vineyards

There was another ranch in Hopland that Barney had an interest in. It was the Shanal Ranch, the vineyard where Sundial Chardonnay was located. After a while, Barney told our eldest son John that he wasn't certain whether he could keep his accounting job and run the winery, too. John told Barney he'd like to help run the ranch.

Barney wanted to make an offer on the Shanal Ranch, but it was sold in the fall. When the buyer, Mr. Matthews, suffered a heart attack six months later, it suddenly became available again, so Barney bought it.

Eventually, John would negotiate the purchase of Valley Oaks with its owner, Mr. Haas, who had lived there for many years, and kept a second home in a hotel in Washington, D.C. When Mr. Haas' wife died, Mr. Haas returned to Washington and hired caretakers to manage the ranch for him. In later years, after Barney had passed away, the opportunity to buy Valley Oaks arose. Mr. Haas contacted John and explained that he was getting older, and didn't have any children. John traveled to Washington and made a proposal. Mr. Hass had a string of lawyers, but John made the deal all by himself. It was amazing how he could negotiate, and that's when we bought Valley Oaks.

Mr. Haas thought an awful lot of John. I think he viewed him as the son he never had. Mr. Haas knew Barney well, so he knew that the Fetzer children had been brought up with a strong work ethic.

Through the years, we would have meetings to plan the future. We'd gather all the children and meet in my kitchen. John would have it all figured out with Mary and Jim. Mary was head of sales, and Jim did a lot of traveling to promote the winery. John's expertise was in finance. Bobby and Joey focused on the grapes, and Patti handled the brochures, wine labels, publicity, and marketing. Everything was done in-house; the kids never sent anything out to be done. We would do it all.

Building Valley Oaks

The Children

John is very conservative, sincere, and always ready to help anyone. He is a good businessman, too, and orchestrated many transactions for the winery. Kathleen ("Kathy") has always been a great help. She loves the outdoors and spends a lot of time exercising. She is a financial planner and oversees the Fetzer Family Foundation. Joey is quite a man. He worked in the lumber business for many years, but later got into the wine industry. Jim is kind of like my father, a jolly, sales-type person, and has always been very good to me. In later years, he did a lot of traveling for the winery, and was responsible for Valley Oaks and how it expanded.

The children were all brought up to know not to get in over their heads, and they paid attention to that idea.

Patti likes to cook and is also an artist. She likes doing things with her hands. She can decorate and that sort of thing. She has always been very close to me, because we did a lot of entertaining together. Bobby is a lot like Barney in that he likes to read and is especially interested in theology and history. I remember, whenever he did anything wrong, Barney would give him the Bible to read. Bobby is a musician, too. He has Barney's violin and can play it as a fiddle. He remains involved in the vineyards to this day.

Mary, the sixth child, is very outgoing. When she was little, she was constantly giggling and laughing, especially with her sister Patti. To this day, I always know when she is nearby, because of her distinctive laugh. Mary is full of energy; she loves meeting people and taking on new challenges. She runs daily and enjoys cycling, hiking, and skiing with her family.

Diana was a little one—even when she was a youngster, she was so little that I was always worried about her, because I could see her ribs. She had pneumonia when she was two months old and I relate it to that, as it took a toll on her when she was a baby. She is healthy today, but still little. Diana loves flowers and has beautiful gardens. She also enjoys antiques, and decorated a room in her home for Barney. I made her a quilt, which she put on the bed, and she has various items displayed that are connected with Barney.

Richard loves horses. He was very quiet when he was little, just as he remains today. He is a pure country boy. Teresa is a musical person and can play the guitar. She was very young in the early days of the winery, but eventually grew old enough to help in the office and work with sales, too. In the early years when we started the winery, all the girls worked there. They did the hand labeling and bottling, and even little Danny would try to help.

Danny is an artist and plays the accordion. He painted a picture of a dog and the kids kept it. Barney told them that they could have parties if they stayed on the ranch, so they got together and built "Big Dog," a large, rustic building that can hold 200-or-so people. When the kids got into the business, we held sales meetings there. When we entertained, Mary would play the guitar, Bobby the fiddle, and Danny the accordion, and we'd all sing.

The children were all brought up to know not to get in over their heads, and they paid attention to that idea. We went at a slow pace, and when we built the winery, we did it piece by piece.

Barney and John headed that project, hiring high-school kids who were John's age. Once, Patti and one of her girl-friends painted one of the building exteriors! In those days, that was the only way you could get ahead. You couldn't hire enough people to get everything done—it cost too much money. Visitors would come and ask, "Gee! Who designed the winery?" They couldn't believe we had done it ourselves!

Christmas at the Home Ranch, 1966

Our Values

I wonder if young people these days know what it means to struggle. It seems that most have everything they want right off the bat! When they get married, they have a home built exactly as they want. They have two cars and take lots of vacations. I don't know that it's a good thing. Young people shouldn't get deep into debt too soon. Often, that's what causes divorce.

I was raised in a different society. Sometimes I hear people say they can't make it without both husband and wife working. If they would just let the husbands work, maybe the wives could learn to sew, cook, and save. Homemade soups are better than fast food for kids. They might not have as many clothes, but they wouldn't have to pay for daycare, which costs a lot. Some wives take low-paying jobs, so they can't be bringing home that much more money.

I wonder why they work outside the home, then.

I suppose a woman can do anything a man can do, and that's fine if that's how they choose to live. Women can also put men down so much that men feel they're not very important anymore, because they aren't the heads of their families. A lot of women like to complain; I thought it was great to have Barney as the head of our family, ensuring that we were supported and that our kids were taken care of.

We are raising a younger generation that doesn't have the same drive. The immigrants had it, because they had to. If you lived on a farm in the early years, you had to work hard. You didn't hear them complaining. I really think that people who are making it together stay together, and are happier and more appreciative than those who are just given everything. I guess I feel that way because that's how I was raised: I didn't expect a lot and was grateful for what I had. Parents don't make their kids work as hard now. I feel so happy that I could stay home and take care of the children. I always thought, I had those kids, and I have responsibility for them. I think that people don't always feel the same nowadays.

I worry for today's youth and for our country's future.

BARNEY

Before World War II, Barney studied business at the University of Nebraska. He excelled in accounting. He was also a good writer, and considered becoming a journalist. He won his state's essay contest while in high school. When we lived in Oregon, Barney attended art classes at the college in Ashland. Later, when he decided to enter the wine business, the bankers thought he would never succeed, but they didn't know how much Barney planned and kept everything in order—that was his nature.

Barney was a quiet man. Sometimes I would see him sitting and thinking. He was a very humble person, and loved people. He was happiest when the children would come for dinner. He would stroll down to Big Dog to listen to them play their instruments, and he enjoyed that, too. He was a tall man with fine dark hair that he always kept combed. Barney was a well-groomed man, and a neat dresser when business required him to wear a suit. He loved music and poetry more than sports. An avid reader, he took boxes of books with him on the ship during the war. He served as a radio officer in the Merchant Marine. I suppose you could say he was a happy-go-lucky sailor.

BARNEY DISCOVERS THE HOME RANCH

One October day in 1987, our son, Danny, discovered this reminiscence, written in Barney's own hand. Barney's love of writing prompted him to write about his discovery of the original Home Ranch.

I found it on a Sunday afternoon in October 1958. An abandoned ranch surrounded by poorly cared-for vineyards in a valley all by itself, nine miles from the Mendocino County Courthouse, yet so remote that it seemed to be the guarantee of a peace and emotional security I had long sought.

The old house was a tall two-story affair, rambling and rickety. Bats and owls nested in the tall chimney. Gardens with lilacs and roses were rampant, and coveys of valley quail fed on the crimson pyracantha shrubs. People said the house was hopeless—absolutely unsafe and uninhabitable. People said the vineyards would not work another pruning or cultivation. Phylloxera had taken their toll. Poison oak

crowded around every vine, and olive and pine oak grew fifteen feet high in the rows.

The old Smith place said, smiling, "Wonder what sucker will take it over? The price is far too high."

I was drawn to the place like a magnet. I pondered. I dreamed. I checked the balances in the savings and check-

ing accounts. I checked the cash balances in my life-insurance policies again and again. I projected. I discussed. I gathered facts. Taxes. Machinery. The future of wine grapes. We inspected the underpinnings of the house, tore boards off and looked for termites, jumped on the floors, drew sketches, imagined what it would look like after knocking walls out, re-plumbing and rewiring.

Every spare moment I had was spent going over all 720 acres of this property. Corners were found. Old-timers talked

24

to, their remarks weighed, and then, usually, discarded. One Saturday I walked to the westernmost line, one mile above the old house, then headed north down the mountain to Seward Creek and down the creek—past huge pools of cold mountain spring water flashing with wily trout. Deer thrashed out of the alder and pepperwood groves ahead of me, then, halfway up steep glades, turned to watch me. It was here, along the creek, in the ageless silence of an autumn afternoon, that I made up my mind to buy the ranch and spend the rest of my life here.

On New Year's Day in 1959, I started trucking tools and lumber to the old house. The ranch is two miles long—a long strip up the valley—and the main ranch-stead is in the center. Each time I passed the last gatepost, a curtain of peace seemed to drop around everything.

I started in January, building an old bedroom wing into a new kitchen, working alone or with John, my oldest son—many times until midnight.

Then we drove the fourteen cold, rain-swept miles back east of the river to our home in town. My dreams kept expanding, but were intermittently disrupted by financial worries and imagined trouble… all our money was in this endeavor and it looked insurmountable. I recalled the many remarks of the people I had talked with prior to my decision. One haunted me: the Smiths never had water. They piped it out of the creek in the summer. Water was essential. It worried me. When I turned the faucets on in the old house, there was a gurgle, then a slow flow of, tepid, rusty, clay-silted water. The old gravity system on the mountain above the house was inadequate. It would not do. A gasoline pump in the creek 100 yards below had to be started each morning and night. Many times it would not start.

So, I decided to drill a well. I studied witching, talked financing, talked to old-timers again. They showed me the multitude of homes—all dry—up every canyon, even dry holes right along the creek, that beautiful creek where water abounded throughout the year.

January and February passed. A family of Mexicans who lived in a small cabin on the lower part of the ranch were pruning—27,000 grapevines, each carefully pruned back to two buds. I leased the pear orchard. The hillsides and meadows were rampant with heavy grass. We bought fifty old ewes—wild-eyed and skinny—and turned them loose. I bought two white-faced cows and turned them loose in the 300-acre south pasture. Bills mounted. Spring came. There was not time for all the work, and soon it would be time to start the long job of cultivating vineyards.

Gradually, I found myself entirely possessed with the project, sleeping alone in the house nights, bringing the three boys with me on weekends, cooking our meals over a Coleman stove in the empty house, waking up at night to hear the rats tearing around in the attic above.

The well drillers moved in, went twenty-five feet and hit a tremendous stream, went another forty feet for added storage, and pulled the rig out. We have an abundance of water. The house progressed. A large fireplace was built in the kitchen. The plumbing was the toughest, and I hated the smell of pipe compound and the patience and time it took to place the pipes. Pruning the vineyards was completed. We took the tractors into the vineyards: two tired old tractors with many troubles—a wobbly old crawler and a temperamental Fordson. Cultivating fascinated me—the smell of the rich, fresh-turned bottom ground, the churning up of the heavy cover crop, the early morning stillness broken only by the squeak of the disk and the noise of the tractor. Here was a place where a man could let his thoughts wander and expand.

Then came April, and the fear of frost on the tender shoots of the vines—and it came. Late in April, the frost whitened the barn roof and covered the vineyards. When the sun came out, the

Farming, like no other way of life, teaches man's great dependency on the Supreme Being— the necessity of patience, philosophical attitude, hope.

leaves had curled black and shriveled, and the people who farm the vineyards took the ravages in silence, many of them not going into the fields to even look. People said we were wiped out, that it was a terrible loss. Then, the hillsides sported their delicate colors—wildflowers everywhere. The buckeye leafed. The black oak took on color. Lambs came and frolicked on the mountain meadows. The quail sang their mating songs. The grapes came back with secondary budding. Mornings, our valley rang with merriment, and the tractors went tearing through the vineyards the second time around.

Farming, like no other way of life, teaches man's great dependency on the Supreme Being—the necessity of patience, philosophical attitude, hope. Moments of despair, but each moment of despair countered with moments of triumph.

So, we were pulled even farther into this way of living, and when Kathleen saw that it was no longer a passing whim, she seriously prepared to move to the ranch—very reluctantly, however, as she was afraid, most unhappy with the old house, expecting her eighth child soon, and downright baffled by this complete change in family life.

BARNEY'S
PASSING

When Barney had business in San Francisco, he would often stop on the way and go over matters with our eldest son John. He'd visit John and, after their discussion, retire to one of our guesthouses in Shanal. On one such visit, however, Barney didn't appear the next morning, and John couldn't figure out why his father hadn't joined him for breakfast. He could see Barney's car and knew that he hadn't left.

Going to investigate, John discovered that Barney had apparently died of a heart attack.

My daughter, Mary, and I had just left for San Francisco to do some shopping. We had a tasting room in Hopland, so John called ahead and had one of the fellows there flag us down as we went by on the freeway. That's how we learned of Barney's fate.

I was in a state of shock and it was a good thing that I wasn't driving. I believe there may have been something wrong with Barney's health, but he didn't tell me. Oddly, the day before his death, he had gathered everyone together in the winery and reviewed a number of items with each; it was strange — as though he was issuing his last instructions.

I miss Barney most in the evenings. That's the hardest time when your husband dies. It's easy to keep busy during the day. Whenever I began to feel sorry for myself, I realized I was not the only woman to lose her husband, and that helped me get through it. Of course, I have all my children, and so many of them are around me all the time, which helps a lot.

After Barney's death, I began to travel as part of my healing. My journeys took me to Australia, New Zealand, and Tasmania. Later, I traveled to Hawaii, Greece, Israel, Canada, England, Ireland, Wales and Scotland, Italy, Yugoslavia, Hong Kong, and the Netherlands.

AN INTERVIEW WITH BARNEY FETZER

The following is an interview with Barney conducted by Robert Benson, who featured it in his 1977 book, *Great Winemakers of California: Conversations with Robert Benson.*

The Fetzer ranch is tucked against benchland hills at the end of a long country lane, the white house surrounded by grassy shade—the winery standing across the way where you would expect to a see a barn. This is one of the northernmost reaches of fine California winemaking, and the Fetzer family seems isolated and self-sufficient. But in no time at all the Fetzers have become major competitors in the fine wine market, their sales multiplying twenty-fold from their tiny beginning in 1968. The Fetzer formula for this success appears to be moderate prices, good varietal character, and sometimes a pronounced oakiness. Though it is perhaps too early to tell whether there is a "Mendocino flavor" or a "Fetzer style," it is clear there are fascinating tastes at reasonable cost in Fetzer wines.

We sat and looked out at the woods while we discussed wine in Bernard Fetzer's comfortable, book-lined study on the winery's top floor. As I was leaving, a middle-aged Austrian couple on a tour of the United States arrived. Their surname was also Fetzer, and they had come thousands of miles to meet their American counterparts whose wine label they had somehow spotted in Europe. The Fetzer winery is not so isolated after all.

Recommended to drink while reading this chapter: Fetzer Petite Syrah.

Your winery is relatively new, isn't it?

The winery was built in 1968; however, we've been here for twenty years, planting vineyards and shipping varietal grapes to home winemakers throughout the United States. I had been in the lumber business, but now I spend my full time in the wine business, as do my three sons and three of my daughters.

Does a small, family winery like yours have an advantage over large wineries in the making of truly fine wines?

In my opinion, big wineries will seldom make great wines with any consistency. In the first place, they can't isolate small, beautiful lots of grapes. They say they can, but you will find that they have mostly 20,000- to 100,000-gallon tanks. We started this winery pretty much as a hobby in the beginning. As a result, we probably have more small fermenters than most wineries in California and we can isolate small lots of special grapes.

For instance, you may get ten tons of beautiful Cabernet Sauvignon off a certain slope. To isolate that lot you have to have a 1,500-gallon fermenter, and you have to keep the grapes separate while they are fermenting, and then you must separate the wine in the aging cellar.

> *We started this winery pretty much as a hobby in the beginning.*

It requires tremendous effort and recordkeeping. If the winemaker at a big winery wants to ferment a certain red wine for two weeks, he finds it impossible. As he looks out his window, he sees a hundred grape trucks lining up at the crusher. He has to get the fermentation vats emptied and ready for the next surge of grapes. Fine wine must be made at a leisurely pace—its making doesn't fit into corporate production schedules.

Barney sampling 1968 vintage Cabernet Sauvignon

The wine business in California will evolve down to two types of wineries: giant corporate-owned factories that turn out jug wines, and small, family-owned chateaux that turn out the great wines. The corporate winery that attempts to make fine wines producing 50,000 to 100,000 cases per year will not be a feasible financial endeavor. You don't make fine wine with people who at ten minutes to five look at their watches and say, "Let's start rolling up the hose, boys, it's five o'clock." You have to have dedication. The small premium wineries have a place in our market, and I think as our young people become sophisticated about wine, the small wineries will have an expanding market.

How many cases a year do you make?

Roughly, 50,000 cases per year.

Was the great wine boom of the late 1960s instrumental in your decision to open a winery in 1968?

I think it was primarily the desire to have an integrated operation, to see our grapes go down the driveway in the form of a bottle of wine rather than in a gondola full of grapes. Another great incentive was the fact that Mendocino County was an unknown region and we wanted to let the world know about our region and what great wines can be grown here. Also, we sold grapes to amateur winemakers, most of them very scientific people—a lot of nuclear scientists, doctors, dentists, architects, engineers—who would buy our Cabernet Sauvignon, Sau-

vignon Blanc, and other varietals to make their wines, and return each year with samples. They believed these Mendocino wines from this far-north area possessed a lot of finesse and quality. I decided if it was their opinion that the wines possessed these qualities, we should build a winery. We started by making just 6,000 gallons the first year, and each year we've expanded.

Do you own all your own wineries, or do you buy grapes from others in the area?

We have about 120 acres here. We buy about 50 percent of our grapes from other growers.

Which varietals are planted on your own one hundred acres?

Mostly Cabernet Sauvignon, Sauvignon Blanc, and Semillon. I felt this soil and climate were similar to the Bordeaux region, so we selected basically Bordeaux varieties.

What is the soil like?

It's all benchland, very gravelly and heavy clay soils, good drainage, and none of the deep loamy soils you get along river bottom.

How many tons per acre do these vineyards yield?

Our Cabernet yields two tons per acre. Another interesting way to put it is that each acre produces roughly 120 cases of wine per year. I think you first start making wine when you go into the vineyard in the fall with your pruning shears. We prune as do many of the chateaux in Europe. Chateau Lafite-Rothschild has boasted that each vine is pruned to yield one glass of wine. Their production is about two tons to the acre. We keep our vines restricted to that level. Of course, in Europe, they have many more vines per acre. Most of our vines are planted six by twelve feet. We find that's best on our benchland soil.

Are the vineyards from which you buy grapes all in Mendocino County?

Yes, we've never made any wine from grapes other than Mendocino grapes. We believe wineries should restrict their crush to a definite region, so they can offer consistency in the product. We will be crushing some grapes from Lake County, which is a region very similar to Mendocino.

Where is the Redwood Valley geographically?

It lies six miles north of Ukiah, which is the county seat. It's approximately in the center of the county.

It used to be said by vintners in Napa and Sonoma that fine wine grapes couldn't be grown in Mendocino County. Now you and a handful of others have probably turned that thinking around. But why were they saying that in the first place?

People are sometimes motivated by one of

It wasn't until the last fifteen years that the growers became interested in fine varietals. But those few fine varietals that were grown here were certainly recognized as being outstanding grapes.

the strongest basic instincts of mankind, that known as territorial instinct! Mendocino's viticultural history goes back many years, but being so far north we were always isolated. In fact, there was no rail transportation to get grapes or wine out of this region in the early days, until 1910 when they completed one of the most difficult rail projects in the world, bringing the line up the Russian River. And there were few commercial wineries here. The Italian families who planted the first vineyards planted predominantly varieties like Alicante Bouschet, Carignane, and other grapes that make huge volumes of just plain red wine. It wasn't until the last fifteen years that the growers became interested in fine varietals. But those few fine varietals that were grown here were certainly recognized as being outstanding grapes. Wineries in Napa, Sonoma, and Livermore bid for the production of this county, particularly Grey Riesling, Pinot Noir, and Pinot Blanc.

What is the climate of the area?

Originally Winkler classified everything north of Cloverdale as Region III, and this hurt the region severely because people really believed that it was a hot area. Later, a weather-recording station in the heart of Redwood Valley produced data that reclassified this particular area as a cool Region II. As a result of its mountains, Mendocino is full of micro-climates. Here in our own valley where our vineyards are situated, at the headwaters of the Russian River, our climate normally on hot summer days is four to ten degrees cooler then it is in Ukiah. The county has a series of canyons that run southeasterly inland from the coast and are like air-conditioning ducts. About two o'clock every afternoon during the summer these ducts start bringing the Pacific marine winds up into the inland valleys. We're in one of those ducts, about twenty-two miles from the ocean.

Is temperature the most important factor, then, in the quality of your grapes?

It plays a significant part. I just read an article in Scientific American by Philip Wagner, whom I've always regarded as one of the greatest contributors to winemaking in America. He claims that climate is the predominant reason for the great variations in wine. I contend that soil plays an equal part, along with cultural methods. Technology can do little to make a good bottle of wine. Wine is primarily a product of the soil, and exposure. Someday Mendocino may be

Barney in the lab

regarded as the Pauillac of California. Wine is the product of the soil, and you don't get good wines in the river-bottom soils; you have to have benchlands to get wines of real finesse and quality.

Do you think small micro-climate areas should be defined and used on labels as appellations of origin?

Yes, we've been doing that for some time. We label right down to the very vineyard on many of our wines. Our Recetti Vineyard Zinfandel is an example, where we mention on the label the vineyard, the elevation, what sugars the grapes were picked at, and other information.

Do you get sufficient rainfall to dry farm the vineyards here?

Many of our vineyards are dry farmed in Mendocino County. We get from thirty-five to fifty inches per year, forty inches on average. The rain comes from November to March, so there's a long dry spell in between. There's a myth among wine consumers that irrigation makes an inferior wine, but irrigation with moderation is beneficial to the crop. We irrigate once a year, around June. Certainly, irrigation after the month of July can be detrimental to the crop, and we do have many growers who practice this, irrigate right up until time of harvest simply because by flooding their vineyards with water they can get more weight when they sell by the ton. This makes a very inferior wine.

How can you control those kinds of practices on vineyards that you don't own?

We don't buy from those growers. We know just about every vineyard in the county and who follows what practices; it's common knowledge who is irrigating.

Can you get your growers to prune as severely as you do?

Yes. You see, we're very small, and we couldn't afford to take even one load of inferior grapes, because we don't have all those vast inventories of wines to blend mistakes out with. One mistake would be disastrous for a small winery. So over the years, we have learned which sites and which growers produce superior quality, and these are the vineyards we have sought out and entered into long-term contracts with.

Is all the harvesting done by hand?

Yes, all by hand. I wouldn't consider machine-picked grapes. I'm sure that the whole industry is fast realizing this; they've been very disenchanted with mechanical harvesting.

Our pickers come like the birds each year. We always worry about whether they'll be there.

Why?

Because you get all kinds of material besides grapes, and you get a lot of immature, second-crop grapes. You just don't make wine picking grapes in this manner. Besides, our vineyards are too steep and rough to ever be machine picked.

Who does the picking?

Our pickers come like the birds each year. We always worry about whether they'll be there. As machine picking becomes more prevalent in the southern counties, however, it makes labor more plentiful up in this region. And the second sources of labor are housewives and schoolchildren in this area.

What do they use to pick the grapes with?

A curve-bladed or hooked knife.

Do you ever pick the vineyard more than once, going through once and getting the most mature fruit, and then repeating the process?

Yes, we do. We pick Cabernet Sauvignon usually in the last week of October, sometimes as late as Armistice Day. Then on our Sauvignon Blanc and Semillon, we go through and pick a second time, after the main operation is shut down. We pick all the botrytis-affected clusters. Botrytis comes naturally here some years.

We always make three or four barrels of excellent botrytis late-picked wine for our family and friends.

Do you think of your wines as having a style that's different from other California wines?

I think the really discriminating taster is a better judge than I. I've been told many times by people throughout the United States that if there were one hundred red wines on the table and seven of them were Fetzer wines, they could pick out the Fetzer wines blind because of the soil and style of winemaking.

What flavors do you get from the soils?

I think we get a very spicy, cinnamon-like flavor in our red wines from this soil, lots of body, big noses, high acids, lots of tannin.

Which varietals do you produce?

Cabernet Sauvignon, Petite Syrah, and Zinfandel in red varietals. Another we call Mendocino Premium Red. It's 100 percent North Coast Carignane. We have lots of Carignane in the county. One of our great problems in Mendocino is that we're heavy with these generic type grapes, especially Carignane, but when it's grown in this region it really has complexity. If properly made and aged it turns into excellent everyday wine. It's interesting that some of the most famous connoisseurs on the whole West Coast have been sure it had other varieties in it. One of them said he picked out definite Petite Syrah in it, and another was sure it was at least half Zinfandel!

That Premium Red is your generic red wine. Why didn't you call it Burgundy?

It would be unfair to the Burgundians to call it Burgundy. People are becoming turned off by the French nomenclature on American wines. One of the greatest impediments to wine drinking in our society is our complicated system of naming wines. That's one of the reasons wine like Green Hungarian is so popular. Everyone can pronounce it!

Which white wines do you produce?

Fumé Blanc and Mendocino Premium White. The latter is a blend of Chenin Blanc, Semillon, and French Colombard. We are also making a Chardonnay.

Barney in the Barrel Aging Room

Are all the varietals 100 percent?

Most are 100 percent varietal unless otherwise specified on the label. Zinfandel has always been 100 percent; Carbernets have all been 100 percent, but we're thinking it may be necessary to do some blending on the Cabernet to make it more complex.

What will you blend with?

Well, we'll consider that more or less a trade secret.

Do you ferment in stainless steel or in wood?

Entirely in stainless steel, all temperature controlled.

At what temperatures do you ferment whites and reds?

The whites at 55 degrees and the reds at 85 degrees.

Do the reds go through a malolactic fermentation?

Definitely. They all go through it without any problem.

Do you start fermentation by inoculating with yeast?

Yes. We use Champagne yeast for everything.

Do you make any wines wholly from the free-run juice?

Not in the past. We have always felt that our press wine is essential to add good flavor and balance to our wine.

We have French presses. Our yields are very low, which is the reason we do not separate the press wine.

Are these bladder-type presses?

No, they are opposing plate-type presses. Our yields are roughly 150 gallons per ton with those presses.

Do you have to adjust acid frequently?

No. We have exceedingly high acids in our grapes in this region.

Do you have to use concentrate them sometimes to raise the sweetness?

No.

What kind of fining and filtration do you give the whites?

Whites have to be fined. We use a minimum amount of fining material. We find we have a great advantage in Mendocino because our winters are cold. We throw the doors of the winery open. The cold nights do tremendous things for clarifying our wines.

Do you own a centrifuge?

No, and we have no plans to install one.

Why do you say that with such assertiveness?

It's our opinion that fine filtration and centrifuges and pasteurization and all the other processes can whip all the good things out of the wine. You come up with a product that is like American cheese: it offends no one, but doesn't excite anyone either.

How do you treat reds?

Many of the reds have no fining at all. Each batch of wine is a personality in itself. Many of the reds require no filtration and some of them no fining. This requires a lot more work, more tracking, and more time in the cellar. We filter some wines just before bottling.

How much time do they spend in wood?

All of our red wines that get barrel aging—one year to eighteen months. I'm a firm believer that that's the only way to age red wine.

I think I have tasted a good deal of oak character in even your Carignane.

Yes, you have. Some of those wines have been in the barrels for eighteen months.

Are your barrels new?

Yes. We add new barrels each year.

What kind of wood are they, and what size?

All are fifty-gallon barrels, some Burgundian, some Nevers, and some American oak.

How often do you rack?

We don't put wine into barrels until January or February; prior to that it's been clarifying in this cold weather I told you about. After that, we probably rack a couple times per year after the wine is in the barrel.

Do the whites spend any time in wood?

Most of them spend four to five months. These are Yugoslavian casks, 2,000 to 2,500 gallons.

Do you think the great California wines are as good as the great European wines?

I certainly do. I was recently at a tasting at the Waldorf Astoria and had the privilege of tasting a number of twenty-year-old California Cabernets alongside some older French Bordeauxs. New York has a lot of sophisticated wine drinkers and I picked up a very definite enthusiasm among them for our California Cabernets. I thought the California wines stood up to any of the French wines. Zinfandels, well made and cellared for ten to fifteen years, turn out to be more magnificent than many of the Bordeaux wines. I think our Petite Syrah will stand up alongside any Cote Rotie or Rhone wines. We'll never make nice Sauternes like Suduiraut or d'Yquem, however, and we'll never make a Riesling like some of the fine German Rieslings. I do believe it's already proven that in a few isolated areas we can grow some beautiful Chardonnay. California premium wines are here to stay, and in the next ten years they'll consistently outscore the French and other European wines in all competitive tastings.

Selling the Winery

The children carried on, managing and expanding Fetzer Vineyards for the next several years after Barney passed away. Eventually, the stresses of working to increase the company, selling millions of cases of wine, and the necessary travel, began to add up. The dizzying growth of Fetzer Vineyards had really had an impact on the raising of our children (ten of them were involved in the business), and the staggering workload affected our ability to raise kids and lead normal lives.

After three years of courting Fetzer Vineyards, Brown-Forman Corporation presented us yet another offer. This time, I told the children that we should seriously consider it, and in fact, we decided to sell the winery. From our perspective, the driving force behind the sale was the importance of our family unity, and as a result, Brown-Forman succeeded in purchasing the winery.

At the time of the sale, the family had grown Fetzer from selling 2,500 cases a year to selling nearly 2 million. It became Mendocino County's largest winery, and among the top six premium wineries in California. In 1988, Fetzer Vineyards was named "Winery of the Year" by *Wine & Spirits* magazine, and won that designation nine times over the next twelve years. Fetzer became best known for its popular Chardonnay, White Zinfandel, and Gewurztraminer wines. Although the winery was sold, the family kept and managed over 1,000 acres of vineyards, allowing us to stay close to what we love so dearly, our land.

THE FETZER FAMILY THROUGH THE YEARS

More than ten years after the sale of the winery to Brown-Forman, and following the expiration of the non-compete agreements, several of my sons and daughters are producing wine under their own labels.

My eldest, John, has launched his new "Saracina Vineyard" with his wife, Patty Rock, and winemakers Alex MacGregor and David Ramey. In the next few years, John expects to produce 5,000 cases of world-class wine made from organically grown grapes. John has completed his new winery and an elaborate system of wine caves on his 600-acre property near the town of Hopland.

Jim has embarked on an ambitious Biodynamic Resort development that focuses on agro-tourism in nearby Lake County between the villages of Nice and Lucerne. This beautiful 270-acre property with a mile of lakefront is home to Jim's new label, Ceago Vinegarden. Ceago's goal is to showcase the importance of plant and animal integration on a farm by incorporating sheep and chickens to help with pest management and enrich soil life, and providing plantings of olives, walnuts, lavender, Italian Cypresses, kiwis, figs, and grapes with two acres of gardens and natural habitat to create a diverse atmosphere. Visitors are able to experience these hand crafted wines while learning the agricultural relationship from the earth to the table.

Dan built Jeriko, his certified organic winery in Hopland. It's taken considerable investment on his part, including the replanting of surrounding vineyards. Danny believes that his visitors will taste wines that will be among the finest in Mendocino County. Organic wines are big in Europe, where supply can't keep up with the demand, and Dan is shipping there as well.

Since 1995, Bob has been developing Masút, two Organic and Biodynamic properties in Mendocino County. He began with planting 40 acres of certified Biodynamic winegrapes in Redwood Valley. Now, with over 8000 acres of land, his family has become very diverse. His wife Sheila, and two sons Ben and Jake, help him manage their organic beef, sheep, chickens, goats, horses, honeybees, vineyards, seasonal gardens, olives, hay, timber, rock quarry and their new wine Masút Pinot Noir. They are committed towards a long-term goal of sustainability at Masút.

Richard is running his Flat Iron Ranch in Redwood Valley. He opted to stay out of the wine business and instead raise cattle and cut firewood with the help of his son Luke. As for the girls, Kathleen oversees the Fetzer Family Foundation, our charitable entity. Patti and her husband Casey have vineyards in Healdsburg and produce wine under the Patianna label. Mary, Teresa, and Diana all stay busy with their families and interests, including art, music, antiques, and gardening.

Today, I have eighteen grandchildren, of whom I'm very proud. As I sit and look around at the vineyards that surround my home, and recall the path that brought me here, I often wonder where their lives will lead. I hope the lessons I learned from my Minnesota upbringing, as well as the experiences and hardships that Barney and I endured, all of which helped to mold our children, will continue to the next generation. That is my fondest wish and true legacy for the Fetzer family.

Barney with Granddaughter Cristina

John Fetzer

Our mother and father taught their children the value of working together as a team, while competing aggressively in business and in life.

After graduating from high school and spending time in college, I returned home in 1967 to assist my father in realizing his dream of building a winery on the 950-acre Redwood Valley ranch that our parents had purchased in 1957. Together with my brothers, Jim and Bob, and a few friends, we erected a winery building in time for the 1968 crush, producing approximately 1,800 cases of wine from our vineyards.

Those early years were filled with daily struggles. Since we had little money for operating expenses, we scavenged discarded building materials and equipment at the sawmill where our father worked as a full-time lumber executive. Because our father spent much of his time working and traveling to finance his love of farming and winemaking, he delegated the daily duties of managing the new winery to my younger siblings and me, yet he kept a careful eye on the operation and on his children. While he was away, he would admonish me to arrive at the office before 6:00 A.M. to await his morning call to update him on the day's activities and on wine sales. It didn't take me long to discover that that was his method of ensuring that I was on the job early; although he infrequently made that morning call, I was always at my desk by 5:45 A.M.

My father's talent for the business side of the wine industry, and particularly his focus on cash-flow projections and tight budgetary controls, influenced the ultimate direction I would take in the business. His passion for numbers was balanced by a talent for identifying and motivating good employees to achieve 100 percent of their potential. At the time of his death in 1981, Fetzer Vineyards was selling 180,000 cases of wine annually. His training served me well when I was unexpectedly called upon to assume the role of chief executive officer that year, and, particularly in the subsequent years, when Fetzer Vineyards experienced double-digit growth. Intensifying our efforts as a family, and enjoying the support of our employees, we were able to grow the Fetzer brand to 2.1 million cases by the time we sold the business to Brown-Forman in 1992. We know our father would have been proud of our rapid expansion in that decade.

One of our father's greatest achievements was the purchase of the Sundial Ranch shortly

My father's talent for the business side of the wine industry ... influenced the ultimate direction I would take in the business.

John in the Fetzer barrel room

before his death in 1981. From this purchase was born Sundial Chardonnay, a brand that grew to sales of 800,000 cases. In subsequent years, we expanded our business ventures in the small town of Hopland to include the Fetzer tasting room complex, the Bel Arbres tasting room, a specialty grocery store and delicatessen, and several other retail establishments. In 1984, we purchased the 1,200-acre Valley Oaks Ranch, one of Mendocino County's most beautiful properties. On it we built the showcase Fetzer Wine and Food Center, which further raised public awareness of Fetzer Vineyards and became a powerful marketing tool. Following the purchase of the Valley Oaks property, we acquired six additional ranches along the Russian River between Hopland and Ukiah. Ultimately, we owned 1,200 acres of vines on approximately 4,500 acres in Mendocino County.

On the Valley Oaks Ranch in 1986, we began construction of a new winery facility that was designed and built by my youngest brother Dan. This was the first of many phases of construction at our state-of-the-art winery demanded by our upward growth trajectory. During those years, my greatest satisfaction as CEO of Fetzer Vineyards was seeing my brothers and sisters and our employees succeed beyond our wildest dreams, and become some of the most respected individuals in the California wine industry.

In 1992, after the sale of the Fetzer brand to Brown-Forman, the family members divided up the several ranches that were excluded from the sale. I retained the vineyard portion of the Sundial Ranch, now renamed Saracina, where I have built an estate winery, including the first wine-aging cave in Mendocino County, to showcase a brand of ultra-premium Saracina Sauvignon Blanc, Syrah, Petite Syrah, and Zinfandel wines. My wife, Patricia Rock, has joined me in this venture to produce upwards of 8,000 cases of the highest-quality wine of which California is capable. In our vineyards and olive orchards, we are dedicated to using sustainable farming practices.

KATHLEEN MARY FETZER

I was the firstborn daughter and the second of eleven children. My very earliest memories of my father were his love of reading and listening to classical music and Italian opera. He was a true Renaissance man; he had that spirit that drives one to increase one's knowledge and improve oneself.

When I was very young, my father would play Ludwig van Beethoven in the evening when we were supposed to be in bed sleeping. I would cry myself to sleep because of my dislike for his music. Oddly enough, I'm a great fan of classical music and opera today. Andrea Bocelli is my favorite tenor.

My father was well read on many subjects and was skilled at asking carefully worded questions that deepened his wisdom. While growing up, we were usually summoned for 7 A.M. Mass on Sundays, and on school days we were dropped off at St. Mary's Catholic Church for 8 A.M. Mass. We then walked down to St. Mary's School. After school, we walked to the public library to read and do homework. My father would pick us up in the evening after work, and he would spend time reading and gathering an armful of books before we headed out to the Home Ranch.

My very earliest memories of my father were his love of reading and listening to classical music and Italian opera.

As an asthmatic child I was rather sickly. When I was growing up there were no asthma inhalers. I remember my father holding me over the stove to inhale steam. Later on, I would choose to dedicate a major part of my life to becoming an athlete to free myself from this affliction.

The most special memory I experienced with my father was the day that we first set eyes on the exceptional property in Redwood Valley that would change the destiny of the Fetzer family forever. On a Sunday afternoon in spring, my father asked if I would like to take a drive with him in his Morris Minor convertible. We drove out to the old Smith Ranch. As we drove up a small, winding country road, we came upon the old Smith House. I remember the property being overgrown, with many wild iris flowers blooming.

As the eldest daughter, I inherited many characteristics from my mother. Among the most valuable are common sense and working efficiently. I grew up with four brothers, whose primary responsibilities were in the vineyards with my father, while my main duties were with my mother. Together, we did the cooking, washing, cleaning, and the routine tasks of raising a family. I was usually in charge when my mother was in the hospital giving birth to another baby. I remember that my dad would usually make a pot of chili, and we would eat beans for a couple of days. Most likely, the reason we all have a very good working relationship today is the closeness we had growing up. Mother had to delegate responsibility, as you can't raise a large family all by yourself.

I have been a student of book learning all of my life. It's interesting to note, though, that good common sense is often difficult to find. My mother has an abundance of this, brought about by her values, honesty, work ethic, strong faith, and dear love for children. I always remember her saying that the most fun she had in life was being with her children. I think my mother looks so young for her age because she has kept herself young by spending so much time with younger people.

My father was many things to many people, but foremost, he was a planner. He always had a five-year plan or longer. He also believed in securing his plan, which is why he believed in life insurance. In his early years he was an insurance executive. My mother always tells the story about when he had just secured a policy on a man who flew crop-dusting planes. My father had gone back several times to collect the premium, and had just mailed it when word came that the pilot had died in a plane crash.

During my father's business career, he always carried life insurance on himself. The cash value of his policies enabled him to purchase the Home Ranch, and, after my father's unexpected death in 1981, his life insurance allowed the family to move Fetzer Vineyards forward, despite the fact that America was in deep recession and interest rates were 20 percent. The proceeds of the policy were put into marketing and advertising, so Fetzer Vineyards could be taken to the next level, becoming one of the fastest-growing wineries in California before Brown-Foreman purchased it in 1992.

When my father died, we purchased a tower house in his memory in the small coastal village of Mendocino, located in an historic district on the north coast of Mendocino County. My father loved taking his family to the coast. He and Mother often spent time at the Little River Inn. Our family used the tower house as an oasis during the 1980s, when Fetzer Vineyards was growing so quickly, and family members needed a break from their hectic work schedules. Each of our families would sign up for their weekend at the tower house. During this time I returned to live at the Home Ranch in Redwood Valley. I decided to sell my interest in Fetzer Vineyards and continue my graduate studies at San Francisco's Golden Gate University, located in the City's financial district.

Later, dividing my time between the Mendocino Coast and the Home Ranch, I began to get serious about running, and after many years of training decided to run marathons. One of my fondest memories was a trip my mother and I took to New York, where I ran the New York City Marathon. We were "wined and dined" by the sales force at Fetzer Vineyards that week, and experienced a glorious week in Manhattan. We celebrated Mother's seventieth birthday at the Plaza Hotel, where the chef created a birthday cake in her honor.

I studied taxation, insurance, and investments and finally decided to move into the new and growing area of financial planning, with emphasis on investment, insurance, and estate planning. I received my certification from

---

I have been a student of book learning all of my life. It's interesting to note, though, that good common sense is often difficult to find. My mother has an abundance of this...

---

the College for Financial Planning, as well as my Series 7 and life insurance license. My father always advised me to study business. I heeded his advice, and by the time Fetzer Vineyards sold in 1992, I was well prepared to take on the responsibilities that were handed to me. When I started my financial planning practice, I was immediately faced with multimillion-dollar decisions. I regularly attended seminars, keeping abreast of the many financial and estate-planning decisions that had to be reckoned with. We were faced with issues of grandchildren inheriting new wealth, estate-planning affairs, and an array of other matters. Mother and I spent endless hours discussing the various means of dealing with these, including our primary concern, how to prepare for estate taxes following her demise. Eventually, we decided on an Irrevocable Life Insurance Trust and chose to establish a family foundation. It was an opportunity for mother to leave a legacy for her family and be able to satisfy her need to give back to society for her many blessings. In 2000, the Kathleen Kohn Fetzer Family Foundation was established through the National Heritage Foundation network. Today, the Tower House in the Village of Mendocino serves as the headquarters for the foundation, and is where I manage my financial planning practice.

One of my mother's most important qualities, one that has allowed me to keep growing, is the strong belief in oneself that she instilled in her children. When the family sold Fetzer Vineyards, and my mother was in need of a financial advisor, the family's attorney at the time said, "You can't have Kathy be your advisor, because she doesn't have experience in dealing with that kind of money." My mother replied, "Yes, she can, and she can deal with it." Thank you, Mother, for your belief in me.

Kathleen Mary Fetzer in her natural habitat

Joe Fetzer

Immediately after planting eighty-five acres of vineyard, the Sundial brand began to show double-digit growth.

I grew up working alongside my brothers and sisters on the Redwood Valley ranch, tending the animals, working in the vineyards, and helping my brothers construct the winery.

Before 1970, I went to work for my father in the lumber industry, later working for him at Masonite Western Lumber Division. My position as log scaler and in log quality control taught me the value of quality, while working for a large corporation taught me many aspects of the business world outside the family business.

In summer 1981, I moved to the Sundial Ranch to take a new position with my family: manager of the newly acquired ranch in Hopland. Immediately, I was thrust into a multitude of projects, such as removing eighty-five acres of Bartlett pears (my father accused me of picking the fruit before it was ready to be harvested), and spending the fall and following spring preparing the land for replanting Chardonnay and Pinot Blanc. Immediately after planting eighty-five acres of vineyard, the Sundial brand began to show double-digit growth, catching the consumers' interest in a new Chardonnay without oak qualities. As the Sundial brand continued to grow, I focused more of my efforts on the promotion and marketing of it, spending

time with salespeople in the marketplace and touring them around our Mendocino County ranches.

In 1988, I assisted my brother, Bob, in Grower Relations, purchasing fruit throughout the State of California and working with 200 growers to help institute and ensure quality standards. I held this position until 1992, when we sold the winery to Brown-Forman, at which time I stayed and continued to work with Fetzer Vineyards. Once again, I had the opportunity to experience the inner workings of a large corporation, which has been a great asset in my growth and in my dealings with the public. I've been able to broaden my horizons and my understanding of the California wine business, and have enjoyed every day of it.

In addition to maintaining my position in Grower Relations with Fetzer Vineyards, I've joined with my brother, John, and longtime friend, Bernard Orsi, to create a new and exciting wine brand, Mendocino Gold. We are focusing our efforts on Chardonnay and Cabernet Sauvignon, whose fruit will come primarily from our ranches in Hopland. As the brand grows, I will also rely on my twenty-five years of knowledge — having walked through every vineyard in Mendocino County — and my close relationships with the growers.

I have also planted ten acres of Cabernet Sauvignon grapes along the western hillsides of my 600-acre Hopland ranch, known as Tonco.

Joe's son Christopher with Preston Alexander

JIM FETZER

At seven years old I was pruning hundred-year-old Mission vines behind the old ranch house. My brother, Joe, and I would climb into these vines and prune using long-handled pruning shears. Living on the ranch gave us the opportunity to experience many things, such as hiking in the mountains and up and down the creeks, enjoying the incredible wildlife: deer, coyotes, raccoons, foxes, mountain lions, skunks, rattlesnakes, king snakes, and many other types of critters. In the creeks, we fished for trout and steelhead up to thirty-four inches long; eels, turtles, and many types of waterfowl were present as well.

We also grew up with many domestic animals: sheep, cows, horses, pigs, chickens, geese, and peacocks. In the fields, we raised grapes and pears, with apples, pomegranates, and figs scattered in and about. Alfalfa, timothy grass, and other hay crops were incorporated into the farm, creating a very diverse environment that allowed the animal and plant kingdoms to flourish.

This early experience set the stage for my commitment to biodynamic farming, and led to my joining plant and animal kingdoms together to build a diversified and holistic farming entity at Ceago Vinegarden.

One of my first culinary experiences was at the age of ten: early in the morning, our father would take all us boys into the vineyards to prune. We would first start a fire, so we could warm up if we got cold. Chuck Donati, who lived in Ukiah, would prune with us. He told us to bring some baking potatoes and he would show us how to cook a "mud-baked potato." Mid-morning we would mix up some mud, pack it about an inch thick around the potato, and put directly into the coals to make sure it cooked all the way through. After fifty minutes we would take it out and break off the mud crust, leaving a beautiful, mud-baked spud.

We farmed organically in the beginning of our farming years, and there was an abundance of insects, songbirds, and other life in the fields. As we moved into the chemical world of farming, the insects, singing birds, and other life quickly vanished, as did the quality of the fruit.

In the mid-1980s, we changed our farming systems back to organic ways of building life in the soil and encouraging diversity in the field. Now, we have singing birds again, spiders and other insects, and an occasional rattlesnake under a vine. The soils have come to life again, and the fruit has shown to produce a much higher-quality wine. We haven't looked back since.

In the 1960s I worked in the vineyards, building the first phase of the winery with my brothers. From 1968 to 1972, I worked in the winery, under my father's supervision, as the youngest winemaker in California.

After spending a short time in Europe, I went back to the vineyards in 1973, returning to the winery to focus on red-wine production, and then on bottling and packaging design. In the early '80s, my father told me to get a haircut and shave my beard so I could go out and sell some wine. This led me onto the path of sales and marketing; eventually, in the early 1990s, I held the title of president when we sold part of the company to Brown-Forman Corporation.

Jim at Ceago del Lago

During my time in sales and marketing, I was responsible for working with our seven divisional offices and our field people in selling, training, and developing sales and promotional programs. I worked closely with my sisters, Mary and Patti, and we developed many exciting and successful programs, and the tools to sell the wine through many channels. In the early '80s I was instrumental in the concept of building the Valley Oaks Food and Wine Center. Very successful in bringing wine and food together, the Center was also a vehicle that tied all of our promotions and point-of-purchase materials together. Also, it served as a place to train our staff, trade professionals, and consumers in how food and wine could come together and expand the knowledge and enjoyment of both.

From 1968 to 1972, I worked in the winery, under my father's supervision, as the youngest winemaker in California.

At the time of the sale in 1992, we were putting together the plan to roll out an organic label—that was the birth of Bonterra. At this time, my brother, Robert, became the largest grower of organic wine grapes, farming 1,200 acres of our vineyards with organic certification.

I've had an incredible and exciting life, beginning with the direction of my parents, and then having so many brothers and sisters to learn from. We always surrounded ourselves with qualified people, whom we consider good friends, and will have many memories of what it took to build the business to what it became when we sold it.

After the sale of the winery, I purchased what was the McNab Ranch, south of Ukiah, and built a biodynamic vineyard that I sold to Brown-Forman in 2001. It has become their worldwide showplace for organic and biodynamic farming.

With the proceeds from the McNab Ranch sale, I purchased the historic Barnes Yard walnut ranch, between the villages of Nice and Lucerne, on the north shore of Clear Lake in Lake County, California. Here, we are building a 200-acre lakefront biodynamic resort with a focus on agro-tourism. This development surrounds a Hacienda-style compound of buildings with vegetables, fruits, herb gardens, grapes, kiwis, olives, walnuts, figs, and lavender, as well as a variety of seasonal plantings such as sunflowers and wheat. Wine grapes will be the primary production crop, with planting of Cabernet Sauvignon, Merlot, Malbec, Syrah, and Sauvignon Blanc. Domestic and wild animals will be incorporated into the project to demonstrate how the animal and plant kingdoms can work best together in an agricultural environment.

We are currently producing Merlot, Cabernet Sauvignon, Petite Syrah, and Sauvignon Blanc under our Ceago Vinegarden label, and Merlot, Chardonnay, and Rosita for our Tule Bay label.

I can only hope that my children will have the chance to enjoy the business as much as their grandparents, parents, aunts, and uncles have. This is why I'm building Ceago Vinegarden, and using all the experience I've gained to take it to the next level.

A very smart man once told me, "We're not here for a long time, but for a good time!"

Biodynamic Tower at
Ceago Del Lago

PATTI FETZER BURKE

In the 1960s, when our family started growing wine grapes for wineries and hobbyist winemakers, we saw the wines made from our grapes win numerous awards and accolades. It didn't take rocket science to see the opportunity to create our own winery, but it did take hard work and sacrifice. I have fond memories of Dad calling upstairs at the crack of dawn, "You live on this ranch, you work on this ranch… let's get up and get those chores done before school."

Downstairs, Mom would have her stone-ground wheat bread in the toaster, bacon and eggs frying, coffee brewing, and pancakes on the griddle. The aromas motivated us to hustle down to her warm, inviting kitchen and huddle around the fireplace. The way she ran the household was truly an inspiration. She not only fed the thirteen of us, but also baked daily for the employees at break time.

She made many of our clothes, too: shirts for the boys and dresses and blouses for the girls. Mom never complained one bit. She loved us and supported us in ways that most people can't comprehend. Many of our friends are always amazed at what she accomplished in raising eleven children. Her secret? Love.

When we decided to make our own wine, we all wore many hats, which included all the duties of the vineyard, winery, warehouse, and office. As time went on, we gravitated to our own special talents. I was blessed to work closely with my father on package design, and became director of marketing services. Here, I had the opportunity to work closely with my brothers and sisters, as well as some of the best design people in the business. I will always value that working relationship with my siblings and the design team. There was always an atmosphere of cohesion and devotion to achieving our goals and deadlines. Many friendships were built and still flourish today, bonded by the trials and tribulations of achieving our family's commitment to quality. Their work ethic contributed profoundly to our success, and I will forever be grateful.

Casey and I are producing wine from our Patianna Organic

"You live on this ranch, you work on this ranch ... let's get up and get those chores done before school."

Patti feeds the "vineyard workers" at Patianna

Vineyards, a 126-acre property nestled alongside the Russian River in Mendocino County (pattianna.com). Patianna's inspiration comes from the tenets of biodynamic farming and our family traditions. Grape growing is an extension of our belief that exceptional quality in wine is achieved when the land, the farmer, and the winemaker operate in harmony. The flavor, structure, and texture of Patianna's wine reflect our progressive farming techniques, which are based on a broad knowledge of and deep respect for the cycles of nature.

Patianna approaches wine growing through lessons learned from my father, who often said, "Many footprints in the vineyard show that the vines are well cared for." At Patianna Organic Vineyards, the footprints belong to me, Kieran, winemaker Steve Ryan, vineyard foreman Horacio Ortega and his field crew, abundant indigenous wildlife — and flocks of resident chickens patrolling for insect pests. Keen observation guides grape growing at Patianna, and farming constantly adjusts to the conditions of the vines, soil, and season.

ROBERT FETZER

When I first moved to the ranch in the late 1950s, I was four years old. From the beginning, I was involved in the general farm work. One of my clearest memories was milking our two cows, Betsy and Babe, and helping my mother make butter and cheese from their milk. My mother would wake me up early in the morning to the smell of breakfast. Along with the two Jersey cows were the sheep. In May, I would help with the shearing by putting the wool in the sacks. Also, I helped with the work in the vineyards, pruning, hoeing, suckering, and picking. I can remember my mother bringing us lunch out in the vineyards every day.

Another treasured memory is of when my mother would get mad at one of us and would say, "Jimmy, Johnny, Joey, Bobby, Richey, Danny…" until she finally got the right name.

My brother, Jim, and I worked in the winery when it first began, but it was always my desire to work outdoors. From 1971–1977, I began full-time work in the vineyards. Also, I worked for a short time managing our wine warehouse in Ukiah.

When I was in high school, I moved out of the main house across the creek and built a small cabin. About a

Bobby & Sheila together at home in Covelo

55

year later, my brother, Jim, moved back from college and built a teepee next to my cabin. This was when the Big Dog complex started. We bought two mini pack mules, Poncho and Burra, and built a barn for them. This lasted a year and then we got rid of them. Having an empty barn, we decided to make it a saloon. Since we always had a lot of friends visiting, we found it necessary to build an establishment. This was okay with my father, since he was adamant that we stay on the ranch when we consumed alcoholic beverages. We began adding annual harvest parties that would last three days, and most of the community was invited to the celebration. This event became a major event for our in-house sales team and our distributors from around the world.

We continued adding on to this complex, widely known as the Big Dog. The name came from Edgar Jackson, a local Pomo Indian who lived on the Home Ranch. While pruning, my brothers and I always gathered historical information about the area from him, and he mentioned that there used to be a Big Dog Saloon in the area. The Original Big Dog Saloon is now under the waters of Lake Mendocino. In July 1990, the original structure that Jim

...my mother would get mad at one of us and would say, "Jimmy, Johnny, Joey, Bobby, Richey, Danny..." until she finally got the right name.

and I built burnt to the ground. The news saddened the community, as well as our sales force around the country. With a major sales event set to take place within a facility that was now gone, we were in a troubling situation, but with the help of the vineyards crew, local contractors, friends, and the family, we rebuilt the facility overnight.

While the Big Dog is certainly much quieter today than in the past, my mother continues to host her birthday party in November every year at the saloon. The Big Dog was a cornerstone of our family business. Brown-Forman, the multinational conglomerate that purchased Fetzer Vineyards later on, made attempts at remaking the Big Dog, but was not as successful.

I met Sheila Solomon in the early 1970s through my sister Mary, and in 1979 we were married. The same year our first son, Benjamin, was born. In 1981, our second son, Jacob, was born. I continued to manage the vineyards until my father passed away in 1981. From that time, until we sold the winery in 1992, my primary responsibility was to secure grapes from large and small growers for the winery. No matter how large the winery would grow, I always felt a responsibility to take care of the small farms in the local community. Also, I worked with my brother, John, in purchasing various ranches on the North Coast and in Monterey County. After selling the winery, I managed all the vineyards for Kohn Properties, which were the remaining properties we retained. Kohn was dissolved in 1997.

Currently, I'm involved in ranching Mendocino County. I manage 8,400 acres of property, consisting of grapes, cattle, hay, timber, and a large rock quarry. I am devoted to organic and biodynamic farming principles and practices. My son, Ben, is currently helping manage our cattle and hay operations in Round Valley, and Jacob is managing the vineyards in Redwood Valley. Sheila is in charge of product design for our wines under the Masút Vineyards label.

It was fun growing up in a large family. We all got along very well, but there was always work, too. My father always said, "If you live on the ranch, you work on the ranch."

Bobby with Young Jake, Ben and Barney

Mary Fetzer

Growing up participating in building a family business was a unique experience. I feel very fortunate that our parents gave us so much responsibility as children and young adults. Our father was the visionary and the inspiration behind the business. Our mother instilled good values and manners, gave us a solid religious foundation, and taught us management skills.

When it came to raising children and running the household, Mother was the quintessential manager. She was, and still is, extremely disciplined, well organized, and skillful at delegating. She was my earliest influence as a manager, and I strove to imitate her excellent managerial skills when I was working. Mother gave me an understanding of commitment and accountability. She taught me to stay grounded, to be a team player, and to rely on good common sense when making decisions. Mom showed us how to work hard, but also how to have fun. She always made time for good, old-fashioned family fun, and we all inherited her love for entertaining, music, dancing, and travel. This balance between work and play kept us re-energized and motivated.

Mom and Dad required everyone in our family to participate in our grape-growing and wine-producing business. During the early years, I helped out in the vineyards and with bottling and labeling wine. In 1974, after high school and a few outside jobs, I joined the business full time, working in production, administration, public relations, warehousing, and shipping.

Dad slowly introduced me to sales and marketing after I had acquired four years' experience in various other positions. Working directly for Dad was exciting and challenging, and it provided me the opportunity to get to know him in a special way. He became my mentor. Our father was a fair and firm man. His strong work ethic set an example for everyone in the family. He inspired us to set and attain goals through determination and hard work. Dad encouraged creativity, responsibility, and decision making. Reaching for the standards he set instilled confidence and kept us thoroughly challenged and involved. Working closely with Dad, I learned about inventory control, distribution, distributor negotiations, sales forecasting, budget planning, and pricing and profit strategies. He taught me to hire talented people and to trust their judgment. He was a great teacher. People respected his wit, integrity, and keen business sense, and were

Collectively, our family conceived the idea of marketing food and wine together to promote a healthy and responsible lifestyle.

charmed by his style, gentleness, and sense of humor. I truly value the opportunity I had in working with him.

In 1981, when our father passed away, I assumed the role of sales and marketing manager. During the succeeding eleven years, our sales grew from 350,000 cases to 2 million cases. I worked closely with John, Jim, Patti, and Teresa, and our sales and marketing organization grew to seventy-five people strong. We established division sales offices in San Francisco, Los Angeles, New York, Chicago, Miami, and Houston. Our team consisted of experienced sales professionals who managed wholesalers and supervised all major retail and restaurant accounts within their regions. I traveled a great deal, both domestically and internationally, to oversee our sales managers and call on major accounts.

Collectively, our family conceived the idea of marketing food and wine together to promote a healthy and responsible lifestyle. In 1985, we developed the Valley Oaks Food and Wine Educational Center to support this marketing campaign. The Center included a five-acre organic garden, experimental kitchen, conference facility, and guestrooms. World-renowned chefs and restaurant and hotel executives visited the Center to educate and share information with consumer groups and wine industry professionals. In addition, we implemented a plan to convert our 1,200 acres of vineyards in Mendocino County from conventional to organic farming practices; we then created the Bonterra brand to showcase wines made exclusively from organically grown grapes. Our family thus became one of the pioneers of organic viticulture, which led to the sustainable agricultural movement within the California wine industry today. We paid close attention to pricing, promotions, public relations, and innovative marketing. As a result, Fetzer became a leading California wine brand.

Mary with Paul Dolan in the Barrel Room

Shortly after the sale of the winery to Brown-Forman in late 1992, I married Hank Skade, returned to school, and earned a bachelor's degree in English Literature at Dominican College. In 1998, I gave birth to my daughter, Kelsey Anne. That same year, Hank, our son, Tyler, Kelsey, and I acquired the 125-acre organic "Kircher" vineyard from Kohn properties and renamed it the "Haiku Vineyard."

Tyler entered U.C. Davis in 1999, and graduated with a degree in Economics. Today, I am fully engaged in raising little Kelsey Anne and involved with our grape-growing business. Hank manages our vineyard, develops land in Oregon, climbs mountains worldwide, and is active in several environmental organizations.

DIANA FETZER

The Valley Oaks plan to include a staff floriculturist created an opportunity for me to pursue a longtime interest and "true love" of flowers.

Born in 1957, the eighth of eleven children, I was working the vineyards before I could walk. My earliest memories are of riding the tractor during harvest and going with my brothers to prune the vineyards, all the time collecting wildflowers for pressing.

As the winery and I grew, I became involved in every aspect of wine production, including managing the Winemaking Lab and the Experimental Winemaking Department. In collaboration with my husband, Wine Master Paul Dolan, I experimented with winemaking techniques including eighteenth-century fermentation processes, barrel selection, and barrel seasoning and cask aging. Responsible for the implementation and analysis, I conducted more than 500 tests that spanned nearly three years. These findings were later incorporated into Fetzer's Reserve winemaking program to assure the finest wine quality.

The Valley Oaks plan to include a staff floriculturist created an opportunity for me to pursue a longtime interest and "true love" of flowers. I studied horticulture and then began a seven-month period of working with Valley Oaks Garden Director Michael Maltase. It was invaluable training. I learned many different methods while applying my knowledge working in a producing garden.

With my Valley Oaks Workshop completed, I began focusing on my new responsibilities. I stared creating intriguing floral designs for the Food & Wine Center and nearby Sundial Grill, using the bounty of colorful flowers from the Valley Oaks Garden, as well as cuttings from my own garden.

In November 1996, my husband, Paul, and I gave birth to a daughter, and in 2002 we moved to Sonoma County. Our daughter is now enrolled in a parochial elementary school.

Diana Fetzer draws a wine sample in the Barrel Room to test quality.

RICHARD FETZER

I was number nine in the birth order. I was born in July 1959 on the Home Ranch in Redwood Valley, California, which is where I grew up. To this day, I live within a mile of the Home Ranch. I began working when I was very young. As I recall, my first duties were mostly maintenance jobs such as mowing lawns, picking up trash, sweeping, and keeping things tidy. It wasn't long before I joined my brothers and sisters in the vineyards. It really didn't feel like work, because we were all together helping make the vineyard produce. We all just did what needed to be done. If I wasn't able to do the job alone, my siblings would teach me how, or help me accomplish the task.

In 1980, I was promoted to the trucking division of the winery. My wine deliveries took me out of the Redwood Valley and Ukiah area to the Central Valley and San Francisco Bay Area. I found this a good experience, as I was again being challenged, and became educated about the world outside of Mendocino County.

In 1986, I finally worked my way into a management position. This was also a challenging time. I was in charge of managing the Home Ranch Vineyard and the Oman Ranch Vineyard. We worked long hours, doing all that was needed to produce a quality product. I looked forward to harvest time, as this was the final proof of all the effort, hard times, and intense labor required in the vineyard operation. I was proud that my employees and I produced high-quality grapes, despite that fact that the elements would at times make us wonder how good the finished product would turn out.

I was married in 1985 and blessed with a daughter, Jessica, and a son, Luke. After the sale of the winery, I returned to the trucking division of Kohn Properties, hauling equipment to the various vineyards, maintaining roads, and overseeing the repair and maintenance of equipment. Later, for a greater challenge, I purchased property in the Redwood Valley area, and now operate a cattle ranch known as Flat Iron Ranch.

One of the things I remember most was my first of many big projects: When I was nine years old, I started building a small cabin on the Home Ranch.

"To this day, I live within a mile of the Home Ranch."

Teresa Fetzer Oster

B orn the tenth of eleven children, by the time I arrived, a solid family structure was already in place. Growing up on a ranch required plenty of work, but the rural setting of the "Home Ranch" in Redwood Valley provided an amazing variety of activities for the nature-loving children that we were. When our chores were done and we could do as we pleased, the hills and streams were always available for exploration and camping.

A lot of responsibility came along with this freedom: in our family, everyone was expected to help in the home and with the business. We were a team, and each of us had individual duties. When Fetzer Vineyards was established and produced its first vintage of 2,000 cases, I was eight years old, and I remember working in the vineyards and helping with the bottling. At age twelve I was given my first "real job," helping my sisters, Mary and Patti, label wine bottles after school, on holidays, and during summer vacations. With the winery's rapid expansion came my promotion to the office. I was fourteen when I was put in charge of accounts payable. Although much work had to be done, we were always surrounded by family and found ample time for barbecues and parties.

After graduating from high school, I married Ken Oster. We built our home on his family's ranch, and a year later our first child, Adrianna, was born. Gibson, our son, arrived the following year. A happy wife and proud mother, I took two years off from the family business to give full attention to my own family.

With the death of our father in 1981, I returned to work in the winery's sales and marketing department. I worked closely with my sister, Mary, in sales, and with my brother, John, on the administrative side. I did a little traveling, but was primarily based in the Redwood Valley office, which made the challenging task of being a working mother more manageable. We all worked to realize the dream that my father and mother founded, and were rewarded with amazing growth during the eighties. As our children grew, so did our family business.

All of our hard work paid off with the successful sale of the winery in 1992. Ken and I began farming our own vineyards and focusing on our own business, Tomki Vineyards. Ken manages the vineyards and I do the office work. We recently started our own small winery, using the organically grown estate grapes harvested

One of the greatest gifts I received from my parents was the opportunity to grow up in a rural environment, where imagination and nature were abundant.

Oster Vineyards wines are harvested from the family's organically farmed Estate vineyards in the Redwood Valley of Mendocino County

on our ranch in Redwood Valley.

My children are grown now; both have married, and both have chosen to follow in their grandparents' footsteps. Adrianna, who earned her B.A. at U.C. Santa Cruz, is now an aspiring winemaker and is applying to the master program for enology at U.C. Davis. She works at Saracina, her Uncle John's winery, and assists with our Oster label. Like my husband's father, our son, Gibson, has chosen a path in aviation. He graduated from the Sierra Academy of Aeronautics in Oakland, has served as a firefighter, and plans to fly in the California Department of Forestry's fire-suppression program.

Teresa, Ken, Adrianna, Gibson, and their dogs

Dan Fetzer

Growing up with five older brothers and five older sisters guaranteed that there was never a dull moment, and I'm thankful for all the memorable experiences I enjoyed at the old Home Ranch in Redwood Valley. The endless open space, with rivers and creeks to explore, fostered my respect for the natural world, which is probably why I feel so strongly about organic and biodynamic farming today. I truly believe that nature is our best teacher.

After-school activities consisted of topping barrels and hoeing grapevines. From an early age I always worked in the winery or vineyards. In my teens, I became more involved in developing point-of-sale materials for the winery: hand-painted large-format bottles for special accounts, murals at the winery, and label design, etc. As a child, I was interested in the fine arts, and my father encouraged me to draw and paint. He was well educated in the arts, and enjoyed landscape painting. When I was eight, my father gave me his easel and a box of paints, and inspired me to exercise my creative energies. When Dad passed away in 1981, I painted a commemorative label in his memory, featuring a few of the elements that I felt symbolized his life: a red rose laid across an open book, with a backdrop of trees and vineyards. These early creative efforts prepared me to design the winery and label I currently own.

I addition to being the winery's artist, I became increasingly involved in design and building there. In 1984, the family purchased the Valley Oaks Ranch near Hopland, and I soon began drawing plans and breaking ground for what would become the Fetzer Winery and Visitor Center. I was responsible for managing the construction team and all phases of design and construction. For the next eight years, until we sold the winery, I spent most of my time overseeing the Valley Oaks project, which enabled my next and even more ambitious project, Jeriko Estate Winery & Visitor Center.

Seen from the west side of Highway 101 just north of Hopland, Jeriko offers a panoramic view of early California and Mediterranean-style architecture against a backdrop of 200 acres of vineyards, trees, and foothills rolling back from the headwaters of the Russian River. I chose the name "Jeriko" (I prefer the original

My father gave me his easel and a box of oil paints when I was eight or nine years old and inspired me to exercise my creative energies.

spelling) because of the agricultural heritage associated with the ancient civilization of Jericho, believed to have been the birthplace of cultivation.

In July 2001, I introduced the first Jeriko wine to the market: a vintage 2000 Mendocino Chardonnay. Now, I'm also producing Pinot Noir, Syrah, Merlot, Sangiovese, and a sparkling Brut. Released in the fall of 2004, the Brut is California's first sparking wine made from organic grapes. All Jeriko wines are estate grown, produced, and bottled at the winery in Hopland. We use only organic and biodynamic practices in the estate vineyards; it's common to see chickens, goats, and sheep roaming the vineyards and hillsides.

My wife, Linda, our three daughters, Ericka, Lauren, and Kellie, and I live and work in the vineyards and winery at Jeriko. I'm thankful to my mother and father for the opportunities they provided me as a child, and for the vision they instilled, which laid the foundation for all I have today.

Jeriko Estate Winery & Visitor Center is located just north of the small town of Hopland. The tasting room and winery are open to the public from 10 A.M. to 5 P.M. daily.

Jeriko Estate wine seal

Jeriko barrel room

Fetzer
Family Album

Kathleen's parents

Kathleen Kohn,
4 years old, being shy

Kathleen – single days

Kathleen & sister Betty

Teen Kathleen

Kathleen & first child John

Sweets

Kathleen's
wedding photo

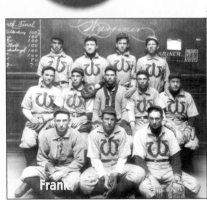

**Frank Kohn, Kathleen's father,
played professional baseball.**

**Kathleen & Bernard,
Oregon**

Front row (left to right): Jessica, Johanna, Jake, Barney
Back row: Katrina, Chenin, Andrea, Cristina, Tyler, Ben

Kathleen in Pete Barra's vintage touring car,
Redwood Valley 4th of July parade

Kathleen & daughters
Diana, Teresa, & Mary

Kathleen with
Prince Pierre Fetzer III
Autumn, 2004

Having wine with
Prince Pierre Fetzer II

THE HOME RANCH

The Home Ranch rose garden

Christmas at the Home Ranch, 2003

BERNARD FETZER

First photos of Future wine visionary Bernard Fetzer

Barney with sales associates

Brothers Jerry & Barney Fetzer

Last picture of Barney before his death in 1981

Barney testing and tasting wines of the first harvest — Cabernet Home Ranch 1968

75

FETZER FAMILY
PORTRAITS

John & daughters Johanna & Chenin

Kathleen and her children in the vineyard

Teresa & Kenny's wedding day

Jim & Bobby in their Sundial Tees

Bobby Fetzer with Jake, Barney Jr. & Ben

Fetzer brothers in the vineyards at Home Ranch
Left to right: John, Joe, Jim, Bob, Dan

John Jay

Adrianna

GRANDCHILDREN

Katrina with you-know-who

Sassicaia

Kelsey Ann

Christopher

Jake

Chenin & Johanna

Benjamin

Andrea

Barney

Katrina

Allison

Cristina

Jessica

Luke

Heidi

Tyler

Gibson

BIG DOG

Pierre II

Prince Pierre III

Poodie with
Kathleen, Ben, & Jake

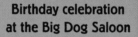

Dancing
with John

The Big Dog was the Fetzers'
favorite party place.

Birthday celebration
at the Big Dog Saloon

Long-time family
friend Charlie Barra
with his good dog

BUILDING THE
NEW WINERY
IN HOPLAND

During construction of Hopland Winery in 1988, the tanks were flown in; the first phase was completed in twelve months in time for the harvest of 1988.
Design and building by Daniel Fetzer.

79

Conversion of hop barns to a bed & breakfast inn
at Fetzer in Hopland

Old Hopland High School is now the
Fetzer tasting room in Hopland.

Once a year, the Fetzers would entertain the National Sales
Force and their families in Hopland and Redwood Valley.
This is the 1990 sales team.

Since 1968 Fetzer Vineyards has produced
a wide variety of quality wines.

Patti Fetzer in
the barrel room
at Home Ranch,
1990s

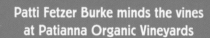

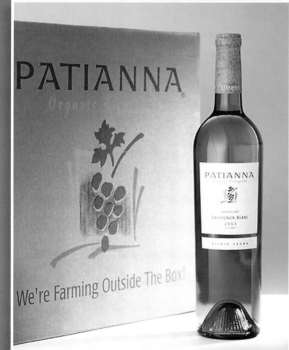

Patti Fetzer Burke minds the vines
at Patianna Organic Vineyards

CEÀGO'S
"KATHLEEN'S VINEYARD"
SAUVIGNON BLANC

CEÀGO
VINEGARDEN

ESTATE GROWN
2003
Kathleen's Vineyard
Sauvignon Blanc
MENDOCINO COUNTY
CALIFORNIA

ALC. 13.5% BY VOL.

"The grapes are from my mother's personal vineyard surrounding her home. Kathleen's Vineyard is the original vineyard developed by Bernard and Kathleen Fetzer over forty-five years ago..."
—Jim Fetzer

Jim Fetzer and View of Clear Lake from Ceàgo

RICHARD AT FLAT IRON RANCH

Richard Fetzer is a country boy at heart and continues the pastoral life on Flat Iron Ranch today.

83

ROBERT FETZER

Masút Pinot Noir Grapes

Bobby's son Jake manages their Biodynamically farmed vineyards and new wine label Masút.

MASÚT
REDWOOD VALLEY
10,200 Bottles Produced

PINOT NOIR
2003

WINE GROWER

Product of Mendocino County

ALC. BY VOL 14.5%

Bobby's son Ben manages their organic cattle in Covelo.

Feeder barn

Henley Oak Tree,
Largest Valley Oak in the world,
is on their Covelo Property.

Barrel Room

Hand-painted large-format bottle

THE ART OF DANIEL FETZER

The artist as a young dog

FETZER
COMMEMORATIVE
BOTTLING

Dedicated to the memory of
BERNARD A. FETZER
1920-1981
founder of fetzer
Vineyards and a family
tradition of fine wine-
making. Barney Fetzer was
a leader in the development
of Mendocino and Lake
County wines and in em-
phasizing the development
of quality vineyards. This
dedication to producing
top quality wines is con-
tinued by his children
today.

1980
home vineyard

mendocino
zinfandel

1980
home vineyard
zinfandel
the first vineyard-
designated vintage from
Barney Fetzer's home
ranch. Grown on hillside
terraced benchland of well-
drained, red clay soil, the
grapes were harvested on
October 10, 1980 at 25°
Brix. The wine was aged 10
months in American oak.
Acid/pH .67/3.56.

Grown, produced and bottled by fetzer vineyards
Redwood Valley, California, U.S.A. Alcohol 14.7% by Vol.

Commemorative Label

Truck Murals painted by Daniel

Wall mural at Hopland Tasting Room Summer 1981

85

Today, Daniel runs his Jeriko Winery in Hopland.

Kathleen Fetzer's
RECIPE COLLECTION

INTRODUCTION

While raising eleven children, I have gathered and created recipes for more than fifty years. As you might imagine, I tested and revised these recipes until they earned my stamp of approval—and the smiling approval of my children, who, as you know, can be the harshest judges.

I created most of these items in my kitchen, and collected several favorites along the way from family and friends. These treasured recipes are a gift from my family to yours. I hope you'll enjoy them and find them as satisfying and heartwarming as my family has.

Kathleen Kohn Fetzer

KATHLEEN'S KITCHEN

Kathleen was a stay-at-home mother. She would have homemade cookies ready for her children when they came home from school, as well as for the many employees who labored in "Kathleen's Vineyard."

Kathleen made twelve loaves of bread every other day when her children were growing up. She would grind her own wheat for her wheat bread, one of her favorites.

Kathleen Fetzer in her kitchen at the Home Ranch in Redwood Valley.

CONTENTS

SALADS & VEGETABLES

COLESLAW

2 cups shredded white cabbage
2 cups shredded red cabbage
½ cup shredded carrot
¼ cup grated green bell pepper
2 tablespoons chopped onion

In a large bowl, combine cabbage, grated carrot, bell pepper, and onion.

Dressing
½ cup mayonnaise
2 tablespoons wine vinegar
2 teaspoons sugar
¼ teaspoon salt
¼ cup sweet pickle juice

Mix dressing ingredients in small bowl, then toss with cabbage mixture. Chill before serving. Serves 6–8.

BAKED ACORN SQUASH

2 acorn squash
2 tablespoons butter
Lemon pepper
Salt to taste

Split squash in half, put in covered dish, dot with butter, and season with salt and lemon pepper to taste. To prepare in microwave oven, cover and set at full power. Cook about 18 minutes in a full-wattage microwave, or longer in a smaller oven, checking every 6 minutes for doneness.

To bake squash in a conventional oven, preheat to 350 degrees. Place squash cut-side down on a baking dish and bake for 30 minutes. Turn the squash over, dot with butter, and sprinkle with salt and lemon pepper. Bake for about 30 minutes more, or until fork tender. Serves 6.

BLENDER HOLLANDAISE

3 egg yolks
2 tablespoons lemon juice
Dash cayenne
½ cup butter or margarine

Blend egg yolks and lemon juice in blend-er. In sauté pan, melt butter, add cayenne, and bring almost to a boil. Add mixture to blender and blend on high for 30 seconds, until light and fluffy. Keep heated over warm (not hot) water until ready to serve. Makes one cup.

MOM'S BAKED BEANS

1 (40-oz.) can pork & beans
4 slices diced bacon, cooked
2 tablespoons mustard
⅓ cup brown sugar
4 tablespoons molasses
Salt and lemon pepper to taste

Combine all ingredients and put in baking dish. Bake at 350 degrees, stirring at least twice, until juices reduce, about 30 minutes. Serves 6–8.

Chicken Waldorf Salad

2 cups cubed cooked chicken
½ cup coarsely chopped apple
½ cup celery, cut into slices
2 tablespoons raisins
¼ cup walnuts
¼ cup Miracle Whip salad dressing
Iceberg lettuce leaves, washed
Sliced black olives

Mix ingredients until blended. Place lettuce leaf on salad plate, then fill center with large scoop of chicked salad. Garnish with sliced olives.

Soups & Stews

Minestrone Soup

1 onion, chopped
1 carrot, chopped
1 celery stalk, chopped
3 tablespoons butter
1 clove garlic, minced

Sauté the above ingredients until soft. Add:
3½ cups chicken broth
1 (32-oz.) can stewed tomatoes
1 potato, peeled and cubed
1 teaspoon basil, chopped

Simmer broth, tomatoes, potato, and basil until potatoes are tender. Add:
1 large zucchini, sliced thin.

Cook 15 minutes more and add:
1 cup peas
½ cup small elbow macaroni

Simmer eight minutes. Garnish with grated Parmesan cheese. Serves 4.

Cream of Broccoli Soup

4 cups fresh broccoli, chopped, or two (10 oz. pkgs.) frozen chopped broccoli, thawed
½ cup chopped onions
3 cups chicken stock
½ teaspoon thyme leaves
½ teaspoon garlic powder
¼ cup butter
¼ cup unsifted flour
⅛ teaspoon lemon pepper
1 pint half-and-half or milk

In large saucepan, combine broccoli, onions, thyme, and garlic powder. Bring to a boil, reduce heat, and simmer, covered, 15 minutes or until tender.

In blender, blend one-third of the broccoli at a time, until smooth. If using fresh broccoli, add a little water to blend (if using frozen, thaw and use liquid from package). Put blended broccoli mixture in saucepan and set aside.

In medium saucepan, melt butter over low heat, then whisk in flour and pepper. Stir in half-and-half or milk, and cook over low heat until thickened. Add to broccoli mixture. Heat, but do not boil. Serves 6–8.

QUICK VEGETABLE SOUP

4 slices bacon, cooked and crumbled
1 (16-oz.) can stewed tomatoes
2 (14-oz.) cans chicken broth
1 large potato, peeled and chopped (1½ cups)
1 (15-oz.) can sweet corn
1 (15-oz.) can lima beans
1 (6-oz.) can tomato juice (⅔ cup)
½ onion, chopped fine
¾ cup white wine
½ teaspoon salt
¼ teaspoon lemon pepper
¼ cup cold water
2 tablespoons flour
2 cups chicken, freshly cooked or canned

In a large saucepan, combine tomatoes, broth, potato, corn, beans, tomato juice, onion, salt, pepper, and wine. Bring to a boil, reduce heat and simmer, covered, 25 minutes.

Whisk water and flour together in a small bowl, then stir slowly into soup. Cook 2 minutes and add chicken.

Topping

Cook bacon until crisp. Drain on paper towels, then crumble. Serve the soup in bowls and garnish with bacon topping. Serves 6.

HOT POTATO AND LEEK SOUP

3 cups minced leeks, the white bulb parts and some of the green tops
½ cup minced onion
1 large clove garlic, minced
6 tablespoons minced carrot
½ cup butter
8 cups chicken stock or broth
3 cups diced potatoes
1 cup half-and-half
½ half teaspoon salt
Lemon pepper
½ cup Gewurztraminer or other white wine
1 cup instant mashed potatoes
2–3 tablespoons sherry

Sauté leeks, onion, garlic, and carrot in butter until leeks are soft (do not brown). Add stock and potatoes, then cover and bring to a boil. Simmer until potatoes are done. Puree in blender, then add half-and-half. Reheat, being sure not to boil, then season to taste with salt and lemon pepper. Add the instant potatoes to thicken. Before serving, add 2–3 tablespoons of dry sherry. Serves 12.

WHITE BEAN SOUP

2 lbs. of boneless, skinless chicken breast fillets
1 jar mild salsa, 16 oz.
5 (15-oz.) cans white beans including juices
1 medium onion, minced
1 clove garlic, minced
1-2 teaspoons liquid smoke, or to taste
2-3 tablespoons olive oil

In large skillet, sauté chicken until brown, adding onions and garlic. Remove, chicken from skillet, cube chicken and transfer to Dutch oven. Add cans of white beans, including juices to Dutch oven. Stir in liquid smoke cooking sauce and salsa until blended and serve.

Beef Stew

½ **cup flour**
I teaspoon salt
½ **teaspoon dried marjoram leaves**
½ **teaspoon tarragon**
¼ **teaspoon pepper**
2 lb. beef stew meat, cut into I ½-inch cubes
¼ **cup vegetable oil**
4 cups hot water
I can (10½ oz.) beef consommé
¼ **cup dry red wine**
I medium onion, chopped
I bay leaf
I (16-oz.) can whole peeled tomatoes, chopped
3 celery stalks, cut into ½-inch slices
2 carrots cut diagonally into ¾-inch pieces
4 medium-size red potatoes, cut into eighths

In paper or plastic bag, combine flour, salt, marjoram, basil, tarragon, and pepper. Add meat, and shake bag to coat with seasoned flour.

In a Dutch oven, heat oil over high heat, and add meat and any remaining flour. Brown the meat, then stir in water, consommé, red wine, onion, and bay leaf.

Reduce heat and simmer, covered, 1 hour, then add remaining ingredients. Cover and simmer 1½ hours longer, or until meat is tender. Serves 6.

Chilled Asparagus Soup

2 (10-oz) pkgs. frozen cut asparagus
4 cups milk
I cup half-and-half
2 teaspoons minced onion
I teaspoon salt
Dash of lemon pepper
Nutmeg

Cook asparagus according to package instructions, then drain well. In blender, combine asparagus with 1 cup milk, onion, salt, and pepper, and blend until smooth. Add additional milk and half-and-half, blending once more. Top with a dollop of sour cream and a sprinkle of ground nutmeg. Serves 4.

Chilled Blender Broccoli Soup

I (10-oz.) pkg. frozen chopped broccoli
I ½ cups milk
I cup half-and-half
I teaspoon minced onion
2 beef bouillon cubes
¼ **teaspoon salt**
Dash pepper
Dash nutmeg

Partially thaw broccoli and break into small chunks. Place in blender with ½ cup milk. Blend until broccoli is very fine. Add rest of milk and remaining ingredients, and blend until smooth. Chill and serve with dollop of sour cream. Serves 4–5.

Quick Corn & Clam Chowder

I cup water
I cup pared, diced potatoes
I cup creamed style corn
I can cream of celery soup, undiluted
I ½ cups cups milk
I tablespoon butter

1 or 2 cans of clams and juice
1 teaspoon salt
⅛ teaspoon nutmeg
⅛ teaspoon pepper
2 tablespoons chopped parsley

Cover and cook potatoes and salt until tender. Add remaining ingredients, heat and stir until hot. Add chopped parsley as garnish.

CHILI

2–3 lb. lean ground beef
½ cup chopped onion
2 cloves garlic, minced
1 large green bell pepper, chopped
3–4 tablespoons chili powder
2 tablespoons flour
3 teaspoons salt
1 tablespoon sugar
1 tablespoon ground cumin
1 tablespoon basil
1 tablespoon dried oregano
1 tablespoon red pepper flakes
2 (16-oz.) cans whole tomatoes, chopped
1 (15-oz.) can tomato sauce
1 (8-oz.) can tomato sauce
1 (6-oz.) can tomato paste
3 (16-oz.) cans red kidney beans
1 square (1 oz.) unsweetened chocolate

In large cast-iron pot (with cover), cook ground beef, stirring until brown.

Add onion, garlic, and green pepper, and cook until vegetables are tender.

Add chili powder, flour, salt, sugar, cumin, basil, oregano, pepper, whole tomatoes, tomato sauce, and tomato paste. Reduce heat and simmer, covered, 1 hour. Stir often.

Stir in beans and chocolate. Simmer, covered, 30 minutes. Serve with French bread. Serves 8–10.

POLENTA AND STEW

This is a favorite of my son, Jim.

1 pkg. polenta
3 boneless breasts of chicken, cubed
1 (29-oz.) can whole tomatoes
1 cup chicken stock
1 cup red wine
2 cups black olives, chopped
6 capers
Parsley
Rosemary
2 cups mushrooms, sliced and sautéed
Garlic, minced
Onion, minced
Salt and pepper

Cook polenta according to package instructions. When done, wet a clean dishcloth and wring it out. Place polenta on the cloth and roll in the shape of a log. Keep warm, and slice when ready to serve.

Brown chicken in sauté pan. Season with salt and pepper to taste. Add tomatoes and chicken stock, and simmer 30 minutes. Add red wine and olives, simmering another 30 minutes. Mince capers, parsley, and rosemary. Sauté mushrooms, garlic, and onions, and add to stew along with capers and herbs, and cook no longer than 30 minutes more. Serve over polenta slices. Serves 6–8.

Hot Meals & Casseroles

Country-style Barbecued Ribs

4 lb. country-style (boneless) pork ribs
¼ cup vegetable oil
½ cup onion, coarsely chopped
½ medium garlic clove, minced
1 (8-oz.) can tomato sauce
¼ cup light brown sugar, packed
2 tablespoons Worcestershire sauce
2 tablespoons prepared mustard
1 tablespoon fresh parsley, chopped
1½ teaspoons grated lemon rind
½ cup Cabernet Sauvignon

Place ribs in a deep saucepan and cover with lightly salted water. Bring to a boil over high hear, then lower heat and simmer until tender, about 50 minutes. Drain, and discard liquid.

Sauce

Heat oil in a large skillet and sauté the onion and garlic over medium heat until tender, about 5 minutes. Stir in tomato sauce and remaining ingredients, and simmer, uncovered, 20 minutes.

To finish ribs, grill them over ash-covered coals, or place them under preheated broiler. Brush often with the sauce, cooking until ribs are well coated and browned, 5–8 minutes per side. (Grilling too long will cause the sugar in the sauce to burn.) Serves 8.

Lasagna

1 lb. ground beef
1 (2½-lb.) can (or 3⅓ cups) tomatoes
1 (8-oz.) can tomato sauce
1 envelope dry spaghetti-sauce mix
½ lb. lasagna noodles
1 (8-oz.) package thin-sliced mozzarella cheese
1 cup cream-style cottage cheese
¼ cup grated Parmesan cheese
1 tablespoon olive oil
Salt
Lemon pepper

In large saucepan, brown beef slowly over medium heat. Drain the fat.

Add tomatoes, tomato sauce, and spaghetti-sauce mix. Cover and simmer 20 minutes, stirring occasionally. Add salt and lemon pepper to taste.

Cook pasta in boiling salted water until tender; drain and rinse in cold water.

Place half the noodles in an 11½ × 7½-inch baking dish sprayed with non-stick cooking spray. Cover with one-third of the sauce, add half the mozzarella cheese, then half the cottage cheese. Repeat layers, ending with sauce on top, then sprinkle with Parmesan cheese.

Cover with aluminum foil and bake at 350 degrees 25–30 minutes. Remove foil for last 10 minutes to brown. Remove from oven and let stand 15 minutes. Cut into squares. Serves 6–8.

Beef Pot Roast

1 3 – 4 lb. chuck pot roast
Flour
2 tablespoons vegetable or olive oil
½ cup beef broth
½ cup dry wine (red or white)
½ teaspoon dried basil, crushed
½ teaspoon Worcestershire sauce
2 medium potatoes
4 carrots, cut into 1½-inch pieces

Preheat oven to 325 degrees.

Coat all sides of meat with flour. In Dutch oven, brown meat slowly in 2 tablespoons of oil. Add salt and pepper, the liquids, Worcestershire sauce, and basil. Cover and bake 1½ hours, then add vegetables and a bit more salt and pepper. Cover and cook 45 minutes, or until meat is tender. Add a bit more water if needed. Serves 6 – 8.

Meat Loaf

1½ lb. ground beef
¼ cup chopped onion
2 eggs
¼ cup milk
½ cup seasoned bread crumbs
2 tablespoons parsley, chopped
1 teaspoon salt
⅛ teaspoon lemon pepper
½ teaspoon ground sage
¼ cup catsup
2 tablespoons brown sugar
1 teaspoon prepared mustard

Combine all ingredients except the last three. Place into 4 × 8-inch loaf pan, and bake at 350 degrees for 1¼ hours.

Spoon off fat. Mix catsup, brown sugar, and mustard, and spread over top of loaf. Bake 10 minutes more. Serves 6.

Chicken and Mandarin Oranges Served Over Rice

Four boneless chicken breasts, cut in 1-inch pieces
3 tablespoon olive or vegetable oil
1 teaspoon salt
1 tablespoon butter
1 can mandarin oranges, drained (reserve juice)
1 cup white wine
1 tablespoon lemon juice
4 tablespoons orange marmalade
2 tablespoons cornstarch
½ cup water
½ cup sliced almonds

Sauté chicken in oil and butter, browning all parts of chicken. Add salt, mandarin orange juice, wine, lemon, and marmalade. Cover, and cook on very low heat, about 25 minutes, until chicken is tender.

Mix cornstarch and water and add to chicken, cooking until thickened. Add mandarin oranges, cover, and remove from heat.

Serve over white or brown rice. Garnish with sliced almonds. Serves 6.

Chicken Casserole

1 (9-oz.) package chow mein noodles
2 (5-oz.) cans boned chicken
1 (4-oz.) can mushrooms, pieces and stems
2 cups diced celery
1 (3-oz.) pkg. chopped cashews
3 – 4 green onions, chopped
1 (6-oz.) can (or 10-oz. pkg. frozen) green peas
1 (10¾-oz.) can mushroom soup
1 (10¾-oz.) can cream of chicken soup
1 cup milk
Lemon pepper
Salt to taste

Put half the package chow mein noodles on bottom of 9 × 13-inch baking dish. In separate bowl, blend chicken, mushrooms, celery, peas, and green onions, and place on top of noodles. Mix soups and milk, pour over mixture in baking dish, add remaining noodles, and top with cashews. Bake 1 hour at 325 degrees; let stand 15 minutes before serving. Serves 4.

HONEY-LEMON CHICKEN

4 chicken breast halves, skinless and boneless
2 tablespoons honey
½ teaspoon dried rosemary leaves
½ teaspoon salt
1 teaspoon prepared mustard
Lemon pepper

Preheat broiler. Spray broiling pan rack with lemon-flavored non-stick spray. Place chicken on rack, and spray the top of each breast. Broil chicken 10 minutes. Meanwhile, mix remaining ingredients in a cup. Remove rack from broiler, and spray both sides of chicken with non-stick spray. Turn chicken over and broil another 10 minutes, basting often with honey mixture during the last 5 minutes. Serves 4.

OVEN BARBECUED CHICKEN

3 to 4 lbs. chicken pieces
Olive or cooking oil
⅓ cup onion, chopped
3 tablespoons butter
¾ cup ketchup
⅓ cup vinegar
3 tablespoons brown sugar
½ cup water
2 teaspoon prepared mustard
1 tablespoon Worcestershire sauce
¼ teaspoon salt
⅛ teaspoon pepper

Heat small amount (2-3 tablespoons) oil in large skillet and brown chicken. Remove chicken from skillet and drain, then place in 13" x 9" cooking dish. In a saucepan, sauté onion in butter until tender, then add remaining ingredients. Simmer sauce (uncovered) for 15 minutes. Pour sauce over chicken and bake at 350 degrees for 1 hour or until done. Baste chicken with sauce occasionally. Serves 6–8.

SIX CORNISH HENS

½ cup long-grain rice
1 cube or envelope chicken bouillon
Six (1-lb.) Rock Cornish hens (thaw if frozen)
1 lb. chicken wings
½ onion, chopped
Dash lemon pepper
1 tablespoon sherry
Peanut oil
Salt
1 lb. carrots, cut lengthwise, 3–4 inches
1 lb. green beans

Cook rice with bouillon until done.

Next:
2 tablespoons butter
¼ lb. mushrooms, chopped
1 small onion, diced
2 (10-oz.) pkgs. frozen spinach, drained

In large saucepan over medium heat, melt butter, then add onions and mushrooms. Cook until tender, stirring often. Remove from heat and stir in cooked rice. Remove meat from chicken wings and add to rice mixture. Add spinach and sherry, and salt and lemon pepper to taste.

Next:

Rinse hens in cold water and dry with paper towels. Spoon rice mixture lightly into each hen and fold neck skin to back of bird. Tie legs and tail together. Rub each hen with peanut oil, then sprinkle with lemon pepper and salt. Place hens breast-side up on rack in open roasting pan. Roast in 350-degree oven 1¼ hours. Pierce leg with a fork: if juices run clear, hen is done.

Place hens on large platter. Garnish platter with carrots and green beans, placing vegetables lengthwise around hens. Serve with cranberry sauce. Serves 12.

SALMON CROQUETTES WITH WHITE SAUCE

1 cup cracker crumbs
1 medium onion, chopped
1 egg, beaten
1 (16-oz.) can red salmon, drained and flaked
Olive or vegetable oil for frying

Remove bones from salmon. Combine salmon with other ingredients, shape into cone-shaped croquettes and deep fry, or into patties and pan fry.

White Sauce

2 tablespoons cornstarch
3 tablespoons butter or margarine
¾ cup milk
¼ teaspoon salt
⅛ teaspoon pepper

Combine cornstarch, butter, and milk in saucepan and stir until smooth. Add salt and pepper, and bring to a boil over medium heat, stirring constantly. Boil sauce one minute, then spoon over salmon croquettes. Serves 4.

QUICHE LORRAINE

Crust

1¼ cups all-purpose flour
½ teaspoon salt
¼ cup butter or margarine
2 tablespoons vegetable shortening
Cold water

Mix flour, salt, butter, and shortening until crumbly. Add water, one tablespoon at a time, until mixture forms into a ball, then roll out and place in pan.

Filling

10 slices bacon, cooked crisp and crumbled
1 cup shredded cheddar cheese
⅛ cup onion, chopped and sautéed
4 eggs, beaten
2 cups half-and-half
½ teaspoon salt
⅛ teaspoon pepper

Layer bacon, cheese, and onion on the unbaked crust in quiche pan. Beat eggs in bowl, add half-and-half, salt, and pepper, and mix well. Pour beaten egg mixture over bacon and onions, and bake at 325 degrees until an inserted knife comes out clean. Serves 8.

TUNA CASSEROLE

1 (8-oz.) pkg. egg noodles
1 can cream of mushroom soup
2 tablespoons flour
5 tablespoons butter, melted
2 (6-oz.) cans albacore tuna, drained
2 (10-oz.) pkgs. frozen green peas
1 cup milk
Croutons
Salt
Lemon pepper

Cook noodles according to package instructions. In a saucepan, bring 2 tablespoons butter, flour, and soup to a boil. Cool. Butter a 13 × 9-inch baking dish. Mix noodles, drained peas, tuna, and soup mixture, and pour into baking dish. Sprinkle with croutons and dot with 3 tablespoons butter. Bake 30 minutes at 375 degrees.

BAKED EGGS

12 eggs
12 saltine crackers
1 cup grated cheddar cheese
6 teaspoons butter
Salt and pepper to taste

Spray muffin pan with non-stick spray. Crack eggs, one at a time, and pour one egg into each cup in muffin pan. Crumble one saltine cracker over each egg, and top each with ½ teaspoon butter. Garnish with grated cheese. Bake 20 minutes at 350 degrees. Serves 6–12.

BREADS, MUFFINS, & ROLLS

STONE-GROUND WHOLE-WHEAT BREAD

3 tablespoons (or 3 pkgs.) dry yeast (always be sure your yeast is fresh)
1½ cups warm water
¼ cup sugar
1 (5-oz.) can evaporated milk
⅓ cup vegetable oil
½ cup molasses
2 teaspoons salt
4 cups stone-ground whole-wheat flour
5½ cups all-purpose flour

Combine yeast, warm water, and sugar in large mixing bowl. Stir and let rise 15-20 minutes.

Add evaporated milk to yeast mixture, then add warm water, stirring to blend.

Add oil, molasses, and salt. With hand mixer, beat until smooth. Then add flour, 2 cups at a time, until you can knead the dough. Put in a lightly oiled bowl, and turn dough over so oiled surface is on top. Let rise to double in size, about 1 hour. Punch down dough, form into 4 loaves, and place in 8 × 4-inch pans. Let loaves rise to double in size, then bake at 350 degrees, 40–45 minutes.

FRENCH BREAD

1 yeast cake
¼ cup warm water
2 teaspoons sugar
1 tablespoon shortening
¾ cup warm water
1½ teaspoons salt
4 cups all-purpose flour
Whites of two eggs, lightly beaten

Combine yeast, warm water, and sugar, and let rise for 15 minutes. Add remaining ingredients, adding the flour a little at a time—if you can, beat with a mixer, then add the rest until it is workable with your hands.

Knead about 5 minutes. Place in warm spot to rise about 1 hour.

Punch down dough, divide in half, and, with a rolling pin, roll into a rectangle about 12 × 10 inches. Pinch underneath the roll to keep together. Put on a greased pan, cut slits across the tops of loaves, and brush with egg white.

Bake 40–45 minutes at 350 degrees; after 20 minutes, brush with egg white again to make bread crustier.

When done, place on rack to cool.

BANANA NUT BREAD

2 cups flour
½ cup brown sugar, packed
½ cup granulated sugar
I teaspoon baking powder
I teaspoon baking soda
¼ teaspoon salt
½ cup butter or margarine, softened
¼ cup sour milk
2 eggs
I cup mashed bananas
I teaspoon vanilla extract
I cup chopped walnuts

Butter a 5 × 9-inch loaf pan. In mixer, combine all ingredients except the walnuts. Beat at low speed until moistened, then increase speed until thoroughly mixed.

Fold in the walnuts, and bake 1 hour at 325 degrees. Remove from pan and cool on rack. Serves 12.

CARAMEL ROLLS

Caramel Topping
I cup brown sugar, packed
I cup pecans, chopped
½ cup butter, melted
2 tablespoons light corn syrup

Rolls
2 pkgs. active dry yeast
2 teaspoons salt
½ cup butter
I cup milk
I cup water
I egg
½ cup sugar
4 teaspoons ground cinnamon
6–7 cups flour
2 (13 × 9-inch) pans

Mix flour, sugar, yeast, and salt; set aside. In medium saucepan, warm the butter, milk, and water. Add egg and yeast. With electric mixer, blend on low speed until moistened. Stir in remaining flour by hand

to form a stiff dough.

On floured board, knead dough until smooth and elastic. Place dough in a greased bowl, cover (greased side up so it will rise faster), place in warm place, and let rise 45–60 minutes. When doubled in size, punch down and cut dough in half. Roll one roll at a time on floured board. Melt ½ cup of butter and spread ¼ cup on each roll. Mix brown sugar and cinnamon, and sprinkle over buttered flat dough. Starting at one end, roll dough like a jelly-roll, and pinch edges together to seal. Cut each rolled piece into 15 slices.

Spread half of the caramel topping in each pan. Place slices of dough cut-side down on topping. Cover and let rise 50–60 minutes. Bake in preheated 350-degree oven 15–20 minutes. When done and cooled 2 minutes, loosen sides and turn out of pan. Serve warm. Makes 30 caramel rolls.

CINNAMON CRUMB TOPPING

⅓ cup light brown sugar, firmly packed
¼ cup all-purpose flour
½ teaspoon cinnamon
3 tablespoons butter, softened

Combine brown sugar, flour, and cinnamon. Blend in the butter with a fork, and use fingers until mixture is crumbly. Put this topping on muffins or coffeecake before baking.

Cinnamon Rolls

6–7 cups flour
½ cup sugar
1 pkg. active dry yeast
2 teaspoons salt
½ cup butter
1 cup milk
1 cup water
1 egg
¼ cup melted butter
1 cup packed brown sugar
4 teaspoons cinnamon
1 cup pecans, chopped

In large bowl, mix together flour, sugar, yeast, and salt. Set aside. In small saucepan, heat butter, milk and water until very warm — 120 – 130 degrees. Add liquid mixture and egg to dry ingredients. Blend at low speed until moistened. Beat 3 minutes on medium speed. Stir in enough of remaining flour by hand to form stiff dough. Knead dough until it is smooth and elastic, 8–10

minutes. Place in greased bowl, turning once to grease both sides. Cover and set in a warm place until doubled in size.

Divide risen dough in two, and roll out into two 18 × 15-inch rectangles. Put one on a dampened clean kitchen towel, with long side nearest to you. Brush dough with the melted butter, leaving a half-inch on the near edge unbuttered and free of toppings. Combine brown sugar and cinnamon, and sprinkle, along with the chopped nuts, on the rectangle. Using the towel, roll the dough toward you, jellyroll fashion; pinch unbuttered seam to seal roll, leaving ends open. With sharp knife, cut roll into 12 equal slices. Place in baking pan, cut-side up to show spiral pattern, and set in warm place to rise 30 minutes. Repeat with second rectangle. Bake at 350 degrees for 20–25 minutes or till golden brown and firm to the touch. Remove pans from oven and run metal spatula around edges of rolls. Lift rolls out of pan one at a time, and place right-side up on serving plate.

Sticky Nut Rolls

½ cup light corn syrup
⅓ cup packed brown sugar
3 tablespoons butter or margarine
1 tablespoon water
⅓ cup coarsely chopped pecans or walnuts

Cook and stir over low heat till brown sugar is dissolved. Do not boil. Spread in bottom of 9 x 9 x 2 inch baking pan. Sprinkle with chopped pecans.

2 cups all purpose flour
1 tablespoon baking powder
½ teaspoon salt
⅓ cup shortening
¾ cup milk
¼ cup granulated sugar
½ teaspoon ground cinnamon

In a mixing bowl stir together flour baking powder and salt, cut in shorting till mixture resembles coarse crumbs. Make a well in center and add milk all at once stirring just till dough clings together. Turn dough out onto a lightly flowed surface. Knead dough gently 15 to twenty strokes. Roll into a 12x 10 inch rectangle. Combine sugar and cinnamon. Sprinkle over dough. Roll up jellyroll style, beginning with long side.

Slice into 1 inch pieces. Place cut side down in prepared pan. Bake in a 350 degrees oven for 30 minutes or until golden brown. Loosen sides and insert onto a serving plate. Serve warm. Makes 12 rolls.

CEAGO'S FAMOUS BISCUITS

Set oven to 450 degrees.

2 cups cake flour *or* 1¾ cups all-purpose flour
1 teaspoon salt
2½ teaspoons double-acting baking powder
2 to 6 tablespoons butter *or* shortening (or combination of both)
Milk

Mix dry ingredients together in mixing bowl.

Add 2 to 6 tablespoons chilled butter or shortening or combination of both. Cut shortening into dry ingredients with pastry blender.

Add ⅔ to ¾ cup milk.

Stir together until dough, then roll out and cut into biscuits.

IMPORTANT: Cut *straight down* with the cutter and be sure not to twist it. Twisting will seal the edges, and the biscuits won't be as light and fluffy.

Bake 12–15 minutes.

Yield: About 24 1½ inch biscuits.

Optional: Vanilla Icing

⅔ cup confectioners' sugar, sifted
3–4 teaspoons cold buttermilk
1 teaspoon vanilla extract

Lift rolls out of pan and place right-side up on wire rack positioned over plate or piece of waxed paper.

Combine ingredients in 2-cup liquid measuring cup (spout makes pouring easy). With small whisk, beat to smooth, thick, but pourable consistency (adjust consistency with additional drops of buttermilk). Drizzle icing in zigzag pattern over each roll. Let rolls stand for at least 15 minutes before serving. Makes two dozen rolls.

SOURDOUGH PANCAKES

You will need some sourdough starter for this one. One nice thing about this recipe is that you can start it the night before and it will be ready the next morning.

½ cup sourdough starter
2 cups milk
2 cups flour
2 eggs, slightly beaten
2 tablespoons sugar
½ teaspoon salt
1 teaspoon baking soda

Combine starter, milk, and flour in a large mixing bowl, and mix until well blended. Cover and let stand in a warm place for 8 hours, or overnight. The next morning, add the eggs, sugar, and salt, and beat until well blended. Pour batter into 3-inch cakes on a lightly greased, hot griddle. Cook until golden brown on both sides. Makes 2½ dozen pancakes.

COOKIES & DESSERTS

SPECIAL OATMEAL COOKIES

Mix together:
2 cups brown sugar
2 sticks butter or margarine
⅓ cup vegetable oil
3 eggs
1½ teaspoons baking soda
2 teaspoons baking powder
2 teaspoons vanilla extract
½ teaspoon salt

Add:
5½ cups flour
1½ cups oatmeal
1 (12-oz.) package chocolate chips
1½ cups flaked coconut
1 cup walnuts, chopped

Spray cookie sheet with nonstick spray, and drop the dough by teaspoon onto sheet. Bake 10–12 minutes at 350 degrees. Makes 10 dozen cookies.

CHRISTMAS COOKIES

3 cups flour
½ teaspoon baking soda
1 teaspoon baking powder
½ cup margarine
½ cup shortening
½ cup granulated sugar
½ cup packed brown sugar
1 egg
3 tablespoons milk
1¼ teaspoons vanilla

Combine the flour, salt, baking soda, and baking powder and set aside. Beat the margarine and shortening for 30 seconds, add the sugar and beat until fluffy. Add the egg, milk, and vanilla and beat well. Add the dry ingredients and beat well. Cover and chill for 1 hour or until the dough can be easily rolled.

Divide the dough in half; on a lightly floured board, roll out each half into a quarter-inch-thick sheet. Cut with a cookie cutter and place on ungreased cookie sheet. Bake at 375 degrees 10–12 minutes. Makes 36 cookies.

Cream Cheese Frosting

1 (8oz.) package cream cheese, softened
½ cup butter or margarine, softened
2 teaspoons vanilla
5¼ to 6¼ cups sifted powdered sugar

Beat together the cream cheese, butter (or margarine), and vanilla with electric mixer until light and fluffy. Gradually add 2 cups of powdered sugar and beat well. Beat in the additional powdered sugar. Decorate cookies as you desire.

PECAN COOKIES

2¾ cups flour
2 teaspoons baking powder
½ teaspoon salt
½ cup shortening
2 cups brown sugar
2 eggs
1 teaspoon vanilla extract
½ cup pecans, chopped
2 12-inch pieces of aluminum foil.

Sift flour, baking powder, and salt into bowl. Beat in shortening, and add sugar, eggs and vanilla, beating until mixed well.

Add nuts and mix again.

Form mixture into a ball of dough, then divide into two pieces. On a lightly floured surface, roll each piece into a 2-inch log about 12 inches long. Lay the log on the edge of the foil and wrap, pinching the foil edges to close.

Freeze the foil-wrapped logs, then remove foil and cut logs into ¼-inch slices. Place on cookie sheet and bake 8 – 10 minutes at 350 degrees. Makes 5 dozen cookies.

DATE-FILLED COOKIES

Filling

1 (8-oz.) pkg. (1⅓ cups) pitted dates, chopped
⅓ cup sugar
½ cup water
2 tablespoons lemon juice
½ teaspoon vanilla extract

Combine dates, sugar, and ½ cup water. Bring to a boil and cook until thickened, then add lemon juice and vanilla, and set aside to cool.

Cookie dough

3 cups flour
½ teaspoon salt

½ tablespoon baking soda
½ cup butter or margarine
½ cup shortening
½ cup granulated sugar
½ cup brown sugar
1 egg
3 tablespoons milk
1 teaspoon vanilla extract

Beat shortening and butter for 30 seconds, then add the sugars and beat. Add egg, milk, and 1 teaspoon vanilla, beat well, then add dry ingredients. Divide dough in half, cover, and chill for 1 hour. On lightly floured surface, roll each portion to ⅛-inch thickness. Cut with a 2½-inch round cutter. Place 1 teaspoon of filling on each round, spreading to within ½ inch of the edge. Top with another round and seal edges with a fork. Place on ungreased cookie sheet, and bake 10-12 minutes at 375 degrees. Makes 36 cookies.

You can roll out both halves to 10 × 12 inches and spread each roll with half of the filling. Then roll up, starting with the long side. Leave the edge without filling so you can get it to stick, using a little water to seal the edge. Wrap in waxed paper and chill in the refrigerator. Cut ¼-inch slices and bake on a greased cookie sheet, 10-12 minutes at 375 degrees. Makes 72 cookies.

MACADAMIA NUT COOKIES

2 cups flour
2 teaspoons vanilla extract
1 teaspoon baking soda
1 large egg
½ teaspoon salt
1 (12-oz.) pkg. toasted chopped coconut
¾ cup packed light brown sugar
½ cup (1 stick) butter or margarine, softened
1 (7½-oz.) jar macadamia nuts, coarsely chopped
½ cup vegetable shortening
½ cup sugar

Preheat oven to 350 degrees. Grease baking sheet. Combine flour, baking soda, and salt in a small bowl. Beat brown sugar, butter, shortening, granulated sugar, and vanilla together. Add the egg, and beat until creamy. Gradually beat in flour mixture, then gently stir in coconut and nuts. Drop dough onto baking sheet by tablespoons, 2 inches apart. Bake 9 – 10 minutes until golden brown, watching closely to avoid burning. Cool on baking sheet for 2 minutes, then remove to rack to finish cooling. Makes 2 dozen cookies.

Peanut Butter Cookies

1 cup shortening
1 cup peanut butter
1 cup granulated sugar
1 cup brown sugar
3 eggs
3 cups all-purpose flour
2 teaspoons baking powder
¼ teaspoon salt
1 teaspoon vanilla extract

In a mixer, cream the shortening, sugars, and peanut butter. Add eggs and beat until blended. Add flour, soda, salt, and vanilla, and mix again. Roll into 1½-inch balls and place on an ungreased baking sheet. Press a fork down on each ball to flatten. Bake 10-12 minutes at 350 degrees. Watch closely to avoid burning.

Strawberry Bars

¾ cup butter
1 cup sugar
1 egg
2 cups flour
¼ teaspoon baking powder
1⅓ cups shredded coconut
½ cup walnuts, chopped
½ teaspoon vanilla extract
1 large jar strawberry jam

Cream butter and sugar together, add egg, and mix well. Mix flour and baking powder, and add to butter mixture. Add coconut, walnuts, and vanilla, and mix again. Press two-thirds of flour mixture into greased 13 × 9 × 2-inch baking pan, spread with strawberry jam, and sprinkle the remaining one-third of flour mixture over top. Pat down top with spatula or fork.

Bake at 350 degrees for 30–35 minutes or until golden brown. Makes 18 bars.

Magic Cookie Bars

½ cup (1 stick) butter or margarine
1½ cups graham cracker crumbs
1 (14-oz. can) sweetened condensed milk
2 cups (12 oz.) semi-sweet chocolate ships
1⅓ cups flaked coconut
1 cup chopped nuts

Preheat oven to 350 degrees. In a 13 × 9-inch pan, melt butter in oven. Sprinkle graham cracker crumbs evenly over butter. Pour milk evenly over crumbs, then sprinkle chocolate chips, coconut, and nuts. Bake 25 minutes or until lightly browned. Allow to cool, then cut into bars. Store covered at room temperature. Makes 12–16 bars.

Apricot-Pineapple Bars

Crust

¾ cup brown sugar, packed
½ cup butter, softened
1½ cups rolled oats
1¼ cups flour
½ teaspoon grated lemon zest
¼ teaspoon salt

Filling

1 jar apricot-pineapple jam
¼ teaspoon grated fresh lemon zest
¼ teaspoon ground nutmeg
¼ teaspoon cinnamon
9 × 9-inch baking pan, sprayed with nonstick cooking spray.

Crust

In medium bowl, combine brown sugar and butter. Add flour, oats, lemon zest, and salt, and mix again. Set aside 1¼ cups of this mixture for topping. Put remainder in bottom of baking pan, using a flat-bottomed cup or spatula to pack down. Bake 10 minutes at 350 degrees and remove from oven. Reduce heat to 325 degrees. Spread filling over hot crust and sprinkle with reserved crust mixture. Continue baking in 325-degree oven about 20 minutes, or until golden brown. Cool before cutting. Makes 1 dozen bars.

Grandma's Lemon Bars

2 cups flour
½ cup powdered sugar
I cup soft butter
pinch of salt
4 eggs
2 cups sugar
6 tablespoons lemon juice
Powdered sugar

Cream dry ingredients into dough and press evenly into greased 8 × 11-inch glass baking dish. Bake at 350 degrees for 20 minutes In blender, mix eggs, sugar and lemon juice. As soon as pastry base is done, quickly pour mixture evenly or cookie base. Bake and additional 25 minutes at 350 degrees When baked, cool 5 to 10 minutes and sprinkle with powedered sugar. Let cool to room temperature, then cut into squares and serve.

Walnut Brownies

2 cups walnut halves, toasted, cooled, and chopped

Sift together:
I cup flour
6 tablespoons unsweetened cocoa powder
I tablespoon dry instant espresso
¾ teaspoon salt

In a medium bowl, set over a pan of simmering water:
6 oz. unsweetened chocolate, chopped
I cup (2 sticks) unsalted butter, cut into ½-inch chunks

In mixer, put:
5 large eggs
2½ cups sugar

Beat together, then add:
½ cup sour cream
2 teaspoons vanilla extract

Alternate putting flour mixture and chocolate into the mixer. Add the chopped nuts last. Pour into a lightly buttered 9 × 12-inch pan lined with parchment paper. Bake 20–25 minutes at 350 degrees. On a rack, cool brownies in the pan to room temperature, then wrap pan tightly with plastic wrap or foil and refrigerate until cold. Cut to desired size. Makes 12–18 brownies.

Date Bars with Chocolate Chips and Walnuts

½ cup butter, melted
1¾ cups brown sugar
2 eggs
I cup flour
1½ teaspoons baking powder
½ teaspoon salt
I teaspoon vanilla extract
¾ cup walnuts, chopped
½ cup chocolate chips
I cup dates, chopped

In a mixing bowl, blend melted butter and brown sugar. Add eggs and beat. Mix in the flour, baking powder, and salt. Add remaining ingredients.

Press into a 9 × 13-inch pan, and bake 10 minutes at 350 degrees. Date bars will rise and fall and become golden brown. Cut while still warm, dipping knife in cold water before cutting. Makes 18 bars.

BLACKBERRY COBBLER

This is a favorite of my son John.

1¼ cups sugar
½ cup all-purpose flour
⅛ teaspoon salt
5 cups fresh or frozen blackberries

In a bowl, blend sugar, flour, and salt. Put berries in a separate large bowl, then sprinkle dry mixture over them, tossing to coat the fruit. Put berry mixture in an 8 × 12-inch baking dish.

Topping

Use *"My Favorite Pie Crust"* on page 112.

CHEESECAKE

Graham Cracker Crust

½ cup crushed graham crackers
2 tablespoons sugar
⅓ cup butter, melted

Coat 8-inch spring-form pan with nonstick cooking spray. Mix all ingredients together and press into pan. Bake 8 minutes in 375-degree oven, remove, and set aside.

Filling

4 eggs
4 (8-oz.) pkgs. cream cheese, softened to room temperature
1 cup sugar
⅓ cup lemon juice
1 can cherry or raspberry pie filling

Beat eggs in large bowl. Add cream cheese, sugar, and lemon juice, and beat until blended.

Pour cream-cheese mixture into graham cracker crust. Bake 40 minutes at 375 degrees. Remove from oven, cool to room temperature, and top with cherry or raspberry filling. Refrigerate 24 hours before serving. Serves 10–12.

DESSERT PIZZA

Crust

¼ cup butter
½ cup sugar
¼ teaspoon vanilla extract
1¼ cups all-purpose flour
¼ teaspoon baking powder
¼ teaspoon salt
¼ teaspoon baking soda
1 egg

Filling

4 oz. cream cheese, softened
¼ cup confectioners' sugar
1 cup whipped cream or whipped topping
1 banana, sliced
1 cup fresh strawberries, sliced
¼ cup fresh blueberries
¼ cup fresh raspberries
1 can mandarin oranges, drained
2 kiwi fruit, peeled and thinly sliced

Glaze Topping

¼ cup sugar
¼ cup orange juice
¼ cup water
2 teaspoons cornstarch

In a mixing bowl, cream butter and sugar, then beat in egg, and vanilla and lemon extracts. In separate bowl, blend flour, baking powder, baking soda, and salt, then add to butter mixture. Beat well until blended. Cover and refrigerate for 30 minutes.

Press chilled dough into a greased 12 or 14-inch pizza pan. Bake at 350 degrees for 12–14 minutes, or until light golden brown. Cool thoroughly.

In a mixing bowl, beat cream cheese and confectioners' sugar until smooth.

Add whipped cream, mixing well. Spread over crust. Arrange fruit in colorful pattern across top. In a saucepan, combine glaze ingredients and bring to a boil, stirring constantly. Boil 2 minutes, or until thickened. Cool to room temperature, about 30 minutes. Brush the glaze over fruit. Refrigerate. Serves 12–16.

Pineapple Upside-down Cake

1 (8-oz.) can pineapple slices, drained (reserve juice)
2 tablespoons butter
½ cup brown sugar, packed
1½ cups flour
1 jar maraschino cherries, halved
2½ teaspoons baking powder
⅓ cup shortening
¾ cup sugar
1 egg
1½ teaspoons vanilla extract
1 teaspoon salt

Drain pineapple slices, reserving liquid. Over medium heat, melt butter in 9-inch round cake pan. Stir in brown sugar and 1 tablespoon pineapple juice. Add water to remaining juice to make ⅔ cup.

Arrange pineapple and cherries in pan.

Put flour, baking powder, and ¼ teaspoon salt in a bowl. With mixer, beat shortening, sugar, egg, and vanilla together for about 2 minutes. Add flour mixture and ⅔ cup juice to beaten mixture. Spread in pan. Bake 40 minutes in 350-degree oven. Cool 5 minutes before running a knife around the edge. Place plate on top of pan, then invert to release cake.

Serve with ice cream or whipped cream. Serves 6–8.

Strawberry-filled Chocolate Cake Roll

Cake

6 eggs, separated
¼ cup granulated sugar
⅓ cup granulated sugar
⅓ cup cocoa powder
½ teaspoon baking powder
¼ teaspoon salt
½ teaspoon vanilla extract
½ cup all-purpose flour
⅓ cup confectioners' sugar
1 tablespoon cocoa powder

Beat egg whites till soft peaks form, then add ¼ cup granulated sugar and continue beating till stiff. Set aside. Beat egg yolks with ⅓ cup granulated sugar, then add cocoa, baking powder, salt, and vanilla. Beat well. Add flour, mix thoroughly, then fold in egg whites.

Line the bottom of a 10 × 12-inch jelly-roll pan with parchment paper. Spread cake mixture evenly in pan, and bake at 325 degrees for 10–12 minutes, until center springs up when touched. Mix together confectioners' sugar and 1 tablespoon cocoa powder, and sprinkle on a damp kitchen towel. Tip the cake onto the towel and slowly roll the towel to form cake into a roll. Remove parchment paper before filling.

Filling

3 oz. cream cheese, softened
⅓ cup confectioners' sugar
⅛ teaspoon vanilla extract
Dash salt
3 tablespoons half-and-half
1½ cups flaked coconut
1½ cups thinly sliced strawberries (1 pint)

Combine all ingredients except the sliced strawberries. Unroll the cake, spread the filling evenly over it, layer strawberries on top of filling, and re-roll the cake. Chill in refrigerator, then slice for serving. Serves 12.

CREAM CHEESE ICING

8 oz. cream cheese
I egg white
I cup confectioners' sugar

Whip ingredients together until well blended, and spread on the top of the cake. Serves 12–16.

CARROT CAKE

3 cups sifted white flour
2 cups sugar
2 teaspoons cinnamon
I ½ teaspoons baking soda
I teaspoon salt
I teaspoon baking powder
I small can crushed pineapple drained (save syrup)
3 eggs, beaten
I ½ cups vegetable oil
2 teaspoons vanilla extract
2 cups grated raw carrots
I ½ cups chopped walnuts

Sift the dry ingredients together. Make a well in the center of the dry ingredients and add pineapple syrup, eggs, oil, and vanilla. Blend well. Stir in pineapple, carrot, and nuts. Turn into a 9 × 13-inch baking dish, and bake 1½ hours at 325 degrees. Allow cake to cool before icing.

DATE CAKE

¼ cup pitted dates, chopped
I cup boiling water
I ½ cups flour
I teaspoon baking powder
½ teaspoon salt
½ cup shortening
I cup brown sugar
I teaspoon vanilla extract
2 eggs
¾ cup chopped walnuts

Butter and lightly flour a 13 × 9 × 2-inch inch baking pan. Combine dates and boiling water, cook 5 minutes, and cool to room temperature. Stir together flour, baking soda, and salt. In large mixer bowl, beat shortening about 30 seconds. Add sugar and vanilla, and beat until fluffy. Add eggs, one at a time, beating 1 minute after each. Add dry ingredients and the cooled dates, beating after each addition. Stir in nuts, and spread mixture in pan. Bake 30–35 minutes at 350 degrees. Serve each piece with a dollop of whipped cream. Serves 12–16.

CHOCOLATE AND PEANUT BUTTER BLOSSOMS

½ cup of shortening
¾ cup peanut butter
⅓ cup granulated sugar
⅓ cup light brown sugar
I egg
2 tablespoons milk
2 teaspoon vanilla extract
I ½ cups all-purpose flour
I teaspoon baking soda
½ teaspoon salt
48 foil-wrapped chocolate kisses

Preheat oven to 375 degrees. Remove the foil wrappers from the chocolate kisses. Beat shortening and peanut butter in large bowl until well blended. Add ⅓ cup granulated sugar and ⅓ cup brown sugar, and beat until fluffy. Add egg, milk, and vanilla, and beat well. Stir together flour, baking soda, and salt. Gradually beat flour mixture into the peanut butter mixture. Shape dough into 1-inch balls. Place on ungreased cookie sheet. Bake 8–10 minutes or until lightly brown. Remove from oven and immediately press a chocolate kiss into center of each cookie. Let cool on a rack, then remove from sheet. Makes about 4 dozen cookies.

APPLE PIE

Crust

2 cups flour
I cup butter
I teaspoon sugar
5 tablespoons cold water

Mix ingredients, form into ball, and cut in half. Roll out two crusts on floured surface.

Filling

7 large apples, Granny Smith, Jonathan, or other tart variety
I cup sugar
I teaspoon cinnamon
2 tablespoons butter
⅓ cup flour

Peel apples and slice thin. Mix sugar, flour, and cinnamon and mix with apples, coating them evenly. Pour into prepared crust and dot with butter. Top with remaining crust and seal edges. Make small cuts in top of crust to allow steam to escape while cooking.

Cut foil into 2-inch strips. Pinch around the edge of pie crust so liquid will not boil out. Bake 45–60 minutes at 375 degrees, removing foil after the first 30 minutes.

Serve warm with ice cream. Serves 8–12.

LEMON MERINGUE PIE

Pie crust

I ½ cups flour, sifted
½ teaspoon salt
⅔ cup shortening
5 tablespoons cold water

Sift flour and salt together, then cut in shortening until texture is crumbly. Add water until you have a firm ball that can be easily handled (dust your hands with flour for easier handling). Place dough on floured flat board or surface. Roll from center to edge until ⅛ inch thick. Place in pie pan and pinch the edges around pan. Prick bottom with fork. Bake crust in 450-degree oven for 12 minutes or until light brown. Set aside to cool.

Filling

I ½ cups sugar
3 tablespoons cornstarch
3 tablespoons flour
Pinch salt
I ½ cups hot water

3 egg yolks
2 tablespoons butter
2 tablespoons grated lemon zest
⅓ cup lemon juice

In large saucepan, mix sugar, cornstarch, flour, and salt. Gradually add hot water, stirring constantly. Heat just to boiling, then reduce heat and cook 2 minutes longer, stirring constantly. Remove from heat.

In medium mixing bowl, slightly beat egg yolks. Stir in small amounts of hot mixture, until it's all added to yolks. Return yolk mixture to saucepan, bring to a boil, and cook 2 minutes, stirring constantly.

Add butter and lemon peel. Slowly add lemon juice, mixing well. Pour into pastry crust.

Meringue

3 egg whites
½ teaspoon vanilla extract
¼ teaspoon cream of tartar
6 tablespoons sugar

Beat egg whites with vanilla and cream of tartar until soft peaks form. Gradually add sugar, beating until peaks are stiff and glossy.

Spread meringue over hot filling in pie crust, sealing meringue to edge of pastry.

Bake at 350 degrees for 12–15 minutes or until meringue is golden brown.

STRAWBERRY CREAM PIE

Coconut pie crust

⅓ **cup butter, melted**

3 cups unsweetened shredded coconut

Combine butter and coconut, and press into 10-inch pie pan, using a flat-bottomed cup to flatten. Bake at 300 degrees for 25 minutes or until golden brown. Set aside to cool.

Filling

2 pints fresh strawberries

¾ **cup sugar**

I envelope unflavored gelatin

¼ **cup water**

2 tablespoons port wine

I cup heavy cream

Thinly slice strawberries. In a large bowl, combine sliced berries and sugar, mix well, and set aside until sugar dissolves.

In small saucepan, soften gelatin in water, place over low heat, and stir until dissolved. Add gelatin, port, and berries. Whip cream until stiff. Fold into straw-berry mixture. Chill until set. Pour into coconut pie crust, and chill until it is set enough to cut. Serves 8–12.

PEANUT BUTTER PIE

Crust

Use the graham cracker crust recipe on page 107.

Filling

I cup chunky peanut butter

I (8-oz. pkg.) cream cheese

I cup sugar

I½ **cups whipping cream**

I teaspoon vanilla extract

I cup of semi-sweet chocolate chips

In blender, combine peanut butter, cream cheese, and sugar. Add the already whipped cream and vanilla and blend at low speed. Pour into baked graham cracker crust. Chill at least 1 hour.

Topping

Melt one cup of semi-sweet chocolate. Add ¼ cup boiling water a little at a time, beating with a wire whisk until smooth and fairly thin. With a spatula, spread chocolate over filling and chill again. Serves 8–12.

PASTRY CREAM SUPREME

This easy custard can be made in advance and kept in refrigerator for about a week. Fold in bananas or coconut to fill a baked crust,* or put in fruit, like apricots or peaches. Also, 2 squares of sweet chocolate may be added while cooking this custard.

½ **cup sugar**

2 tablespoons flour

2 tablespoon cornstarch

2 eggs

3 cups milk

2 teaspoons vanilla extract

In a large bowl, mix together sugar, flour, cornstarch, and eggs, using a fork to combine. Pour milk into a large saucepan and bring to a boil. Gradually stir half the hot milk into egg mixture, whisking constantly. Add the milk and egg mixture back into saucepan. Cook, whisking over medium heat, until bubbly and thick, about 5 minutes. Remove from heat and add vanilla. Whisk an additional 5 minutes to cool down. Pour into crust or save in refrigerator. Makes 4 cups.

---

* For a pre-baked pie crust, use for "My Favorite Pie Crust" recipe, next page.

Vanilla Wafer Crust

¼ cup butter
I teaspoon vanilla extract
I ⅔ cups vanilla wafers, crushed
¼ cup light brown sugar, firmly packed

Melt butter. Stir in vanilla, crushed wafers, and brown sugar. Mix, then press into 9-inch pie tin. Bake 10 minutes in 350 degree oven or until golden brown. Cool.

All-American Pie Crust

2½ cups all-purpose flour
2 teaspoons sugar
I stick cold shortening, cut into ½-inch slices
6 tablespoon cold water

Mix all ingredients together, being careful not to overwork the dough. A light touch, and chilling the dough before rolling it out, will work best.

My Favorite Pie Crust

2 cups all-purpose flour
I teaspoon salt
I tablespoon vinegar

I cup shortening
⅓ cup milk

(This recipe makes two crusts, but you'll use only one for the cobbler.)

Put flour, salt, and shortening in a food processor and mix, then add milk and vinegar and blend. (You can also mix this dough using a hand-held pastry-dough blender.)

With your hands, bring dough together into a ball and press flat. (Divide dough in two, reserving half.) Cool in refrigerator, then use rolling pin to roll out one crust to the size of the pan. Place crust on top of berry mixture, and flute the edges around the baking dish. Cut a strip of foil to cover the edges of the crust. Bake at 350 degrees for 25 minutes, then remove foil and bake 25–30 minutes or until crust is golden brown. Remove from oven and allow to cool. Place a serving in a bowl and top with vanilla ice cream. Serves 8–12.

Double Pie Crust

3 cups flour, sifted
I cup vegetable shortening
Dash salt
6 tablespoons very cold water

Combine flour, salt, and shortening in large mixing bowl, and mix with pastry blender or fork until crumbly.

Mix in a little water at a time until the dough can be formed into a ball. Flatten the dough and divide in two. Roll out each half slightly larger than pie pan. Gently place flattened dough in pan, pinch edges with thumb and forefinger, and prick the crust along the bottom and sides. Cut aluminum foil into 2-inch strips and gently place around the outer edges of crust to avoid burning. Bake 12 minutes at 450 degrees. Remove foil after 6 minutes and continue baking until golden brown. Makes 2 single crusts.

Simple Tart Crust

I cup all-purpose flour
I teaspoon sugar
Pinch of salt
7 tablespoons cold butter, cut into slices
2 tablespoons cold water

In a food processor, using metal "S" blade, pulse to combine flour, sugar, and salt. Add a pat of butter and pulse briefly, just until mixture resembles coarse meal. Add the water, and pulse a few times until pastry holds together when pressed. Transfer to work surface. Wrap in plastic. Chill 30 minutes or refrigerate up to 2 days. Makes 1 nine-inch crust.

To pre-bake crust:

Heat oven to 350 degrees. Press the pastry dough evenly into a tart pan. Line the tart with parchment paper or aluminum foil and fill with beans or pie weights. Bake till crust is firm and set, about 20 minutes. Remove beans and paper. Prick bottom of crust so it doesn't puff. Continue baking until well browned, 10–15 minutes. Cool before filling.

Crumble Topping

⅓ **cup brown sugar**
¼ **cup (½ stick) butter**
1 teaspoon cinnamon
Pinch of nutmeg
Pinch of salt
¾ **cup all purpose flour**

Cream together sugar, butter, cinnamon, nutmeg, and salt until fluffy. Gently mix in flour until crumbly.

CHRISTMAS AT THE HOME RANCH

Christmas entertaining at the Home Ranch in Redwood Valley is a festive event where the Fetzer family enjoys delicious holiday cooking and wonderful Fetzer wines. Fetzer Valley Oaks Gewurztraminer is one of Kathleen's favorite wines. It is often called "gavurtz," meaning "spicy" in German, because it is hard to say, and even harder to spell.

WINE PAIRING

Here are some wines the Fetzer family recommends to go with Kathleen's recipes. Each wine was selected to complement the dishes and enhance the flavors of the recipes.

CEAGO

1 "Kathleen's Vineyard" Sauvignon Blanc
Cream of Broccoli Soup (91); Chilled Asparagus Soup (93); Chilled Blender Broccoli Soup (93); Baked Eggs (99)

2 Chardonnay
Quick Corn & Clam Chowder (93); White Bean Soup (92);
Six Cornish Hens (97); Tuna Casserole (98)

FETZER

3 Sauvignon Blanc
Quick Vegetable Soup (92); Honey-Lemon Chicken (97)

4 Sundial Chardonnay
Quick Corn & Clam Chowder (93); Chicken Casserole (96); Salmon Croquettes with White Sauce (98);

5 Valley Oaks Gewurtztraminer
Chicken and Mandarin Oranges (96); Honey-Lemon Chicken (97);

6 Valley Oaks Cabernet or Zinfandel
Minestrone Soup (91)

JERIKO

7 Chardonnay
Polenta and Stew (94)

8 2002 Pinot Noir
Oven Barbecued Chicken (97)

9 Pinot Noir Rosé
White Bean Soup (92); Salmon Croquettes with White Sauce (98)

10 Sangiovese
Beef Stew (93)

MASŪT

11 2002 Pinot Noir
Hot Potato and Leek Soup (92); Chili (94)

PATTIANNA

12 Sauvignon Blanc
Cream of Broccoli Soup (91); Quick Vegetable Soup (92); Hot Potato and Leek Soup (92); Chilled Asparagus Soup (93); Chilled Blender Broccoli Soup (93); Quiche Lorraine (98)

13 Syrah
Beef Pot Roast (96)

SARACINA

14 Sauvignon Blanc
Cream of Broccoli Soup (91); Chilled Asparagus Soup (93); Chilled Blender Broccoli Soup (93); Quiche Lorraine (98)

15 Syrah
Meat Loaf (96)

16 Zinfandel
Country-style Barbecued Ribs (93); Lasagne (95)

SUBJECT INDEX

Page references in italics refer to photographs.

RECIPE INDEX